Managing Extreme Behaviours in the Early Years

Angela Glenn,
Alicia Helps and
Jacquie Cousins

Routledge
Taylor & Francis Group

LONDON AND NEW YORK

First published 2009
by Routledge
2 Park Square, Milton Park, Abingdon, Oxon OX14 4RN

Simultaneously published in the USA and Canada
by Routledge
270 Madison Avenue, New York, NY 10016

Routledge is an imprint of the Taylor & Francis Group, an informa business

© 2009 Angela Glenn, Alicia Helps and Jacquie Cousins

Typeset in Times New Roman by Prepress Projects Ltd, Perth, UK
Printed and bound in Great Britain by MPG Books Ltd, Bodmin

British Library Cataloguing in Publication Data
A catalogue record for this book is available from the British Library

Library of Congress Cataloging in Publication Data
Glenn, Angela.
Managing extreme behaviours in the early years / Angela Glenn, Alicia Helps, and Jacquie Cousins.
p. cm. — (Tried and tested)
1. Problem children—Education (Preschool)—England—Medway. 2. Education, Preschool—England—Medway. I. Helps, Alicia. II. Cousins, Jacquie. III. Title.
LC4803.G72M434 2009
649′.153—dc22
2008025222

ISBN 10: 0-415-46709-8 (pbk)

ISBN 13: 978-0-415-46709-4 (pbk)

Ext| |rs

Tried and Tested Series

Written for practitioners who work in pre-school settings and parents, this highly practical series teaches how to respond instantly and effectively to problems using hands-on strategies.

Other titles available:

Play and Learning in the Early Years
Angela Glenn, Jacquie Cousins and Alicia Helps
978-1-84312-336-1

Ready to Read and Write in the Early Years
Angela Glenn, Jacquie Cousins and Alicia Helps
978-1-84312-337-8

Removing Barriers to Learning in the Early Years
Angela Glenn, Jacquie Cousins and Alicia Helps
978-1-84312-338-5

Behaviour in the Early Years
Angela Glenn, Jacquie Cousins and Alicia Helps
978-1-84312-104-6

CONTENTS

ACKNOWLEDGEMENTS

We would like to thank:

- colleagues in pre-schools, nurseries, foundation units and schools in Medway for their support and encouragement;
- Tony Faulkner for encouraging and useful comments in his review of our book proposal;
- staff at Routledge Education, especially Sophie Thomson and Monika Lee for their hard work, help and support in creating this latest book in the Tried and Tested series;
- Sarah Glenn (Student, BA Hons Photography, University College for the Creative Arts, Maidstone) for doing the illustrations.

INTRODUCTION

As with the other titles in this series, this book has been written in response to requests and comments from practitioners working with young children. In our first book, *Behaviour in the Early Years*, we tried to address the most commonly occurring behaviours encountered by staff working in pre-schools and in school-based nurseries and attempted to suggest some strategies that could work. These strategies had been 'tried and tested' and shown to be effective with most children when delivered in a consistent 'firm but fair' style. These strategies may not always work or may take a significantly longer period to work with children demonstrating more serious or more extreme behavioural difficulties. A different approach, the involvement of multiple agencies and an agreed plan of action may all need to be considered.

It appears that more children are presenting with behavioural disorders and difficulties at a younger age than ever before. Our own authority is receiving a growing number of referrals to support services for an increasing number of very young children with behavioural difficulties. Indeed, conversations with paediatricians and anecdotal evidence from therapists, teachers and parents would seem to bear this out.

From our experience, the behaviours that we would normally have expected to see in older children and adolescents are now being seen in the very young child and even in pre-school children. Hence a headline in a national newspaper dated 21 May 2008 reads 'School sin bins for children aged five' and a previous headline, 'Primary schools suspend 1000 under-sixes for bad behaviour'. There are now many books, television programmes and services available on the subject of parenting. There seems to be a plethora of books, articles and television programmes devoted to managing children's behaviour and some of the fashionable advice currently being aired, e.g. praise wanted or 'good' behaviour and ignore the 'bad', is being viewed with reverence by some families. Commonsense, practical advice from extended families seems to be being sidelined by a growing number of parents who call in the 'professionals'. Recent research backs up the claims of teachers, authors and scientists who blame a range of modern ills for depriving children of a well balanced childhood. The media highlights ideas about poor diet, modern technologies, the sexualisation of ever younger children, the idea of instant gratification and rights over responsibilities. Very young children are being asked their opinions and given choices about all kinds of issues affecting them without the prior knowledge, maturity or experience to be able to give a considered answer. At the same time, children are being taught that the world is a 'dangerous' place and consequently spend little time outdoors, allowed to explore without the constant, close supervision of an adult. Children are put under pressure at younger and younger ages. We assess and test children as soon as they begin their education in our schools and nurseries at three years old.

Television is thought to be a major influence on the developing mind. Some programmes directed at children employ rapid changes of image, complex fast moving ideas that are accompanied by hyperactive presenters who give the impression that, unless they deliver scripts at speed and loudly, then the message simply won't 'go in'. It would appear that the attention and listening skills of children are judged to be measured in seconds. Children who spend hours per day seated in front of a computer screen may be developing excellent visual discriminatory skills and be able to interact using networking sites but flounder when expected to communicate in the real world, face to face. Television and advertising appear to have the effect of 'speeding up' childhood, introducing adult themes to a younger and younger audience. This seems to be having alarming effects. Children as young as seven or eight years are concerned about their weight and girls in particular are altering their eating patterns in order to attempts to fit into a desired 'ideal' body shape. Paradoxically, we have what the media are referring to as an obesity 'epidemic'.

The most important influence upon the mind of a developing child is of course his parents. Helping children to manage their behaviour cannot be done without the involvement, commitment and support of parents/carers. Ideally, this means that service providers who become involved with a child will be required to support the family as a whole. We will examine how practitioners can help to set this in motion. Parents and teachers have anxieties about exam results. From a very young age, our children are expected to respond to a curriculum that is seen by some educationalists and parents as a limit to creativity and enthusiasm. At the same time, parents and teachers often reinforce the idea that, if children do not succeed with tests, then undesirable consequences follow.

What happens to the child who cannot conform to the raised expectations that are inevitable when the 'system' is in force? Some children almost immediately set themselves apart from the expected 'norm' when they attend an early years setting. The regular managing strategies that are in place do not work for this group of children. It has been recognised that children with social, emotional and behavioural difficulties are not able to make progress in what used to be called 'child-centred' education. This style of teaching and learning took for granted the ability of the child to organise itself. Current methods of teaching and learning in our foundation units include child-initiated learning. The implications of this for children with SEBD are enormous.

In this book, we will explore some of the reasons for extreme behaviours demonstrated by young children.

We will explain anger in young children and some of the methods adults can use to deal with it. We will describe some of the extreme behaviours we have encountered and set out some case studies and some possible strategies for dealing with these. The case studies are taken from real cases, the names and details of which have been changed to protect the identity of individuals. We will attempt to provide some ideas about good practice and how to manage aggression.

A book such as this cannot possibly offer in-depth study or explanations but, rather, is intended to give an insight and offer some strategies for a growing number of children with significant behavioural difficulties. It can be very difficult to decide what to do when faced with a young person who is angry and distressed and does not have the necessary language ability to communicate this verbally. It can be difficult for a practitioner to decide whether behaviour in a young child is attributable to its developmental level and which behaviours should be considered serious enough to warrant further actions. We hope the material contained in this book will begin to address this and provide some possible reasons for extreme behaviours. We hope the strategies suggested will help although the very nature of more extreme behaviours would suggest that there will be no 'quick fixes' but that longer-term remedies in the form of management, care, support from multiple agencies, therapies and medications may be necessary.

(We have used the convention of referring to the child as 'him' and the practitioner as 'her' purely in order to avoid clumsiness in the text. This is not to suggest that children with behaviour difficulties are always boys, or that staff are always women.)

What do we mean by extreme behaviours?

Introduction

All behaviour is communication.

Children with limited verbal skills will still be expressing their emotions mainly through their actions, which will need to be carefully observed and monitored to establish the intention. Even those children with good verbal skills will resort to this very basic form of communication when they become emotionally charged.

Extreme negative behaviours occur when the child loses control or appears to lose control over a situation. This is mainly exhibited as highly aggressive, defiant and destructive behaviour. This extreme behaviour can also show itself in a depressive form in which the child tries to maintain some level of control over his emotions. This can exhibit itself in such areas as eating disorders, constantly hiding away in small spaces or maintaining that they no longer want to live.

Managing children in these highly emotional states can prove to be an incredible challenge for many adults, as it is often difficult to remain detached from the child's behaviour. In some cases these children can create tremendous tension in the adults around them. The crucial aspect is that these extreme behaviours need to be dealt with so the child can be supported emotionally.

Today's young children are being increasingly exposed to the adult world via inappropriate television viewing and games consoles. Younger children are developing conditions more typical of older children or adolescents. These include such things as expression of greater violence, overt sexualised behaviour and constant swearing.

There is now a growing awareness of various medical conditions such as ADHD (Attention Deficit Hyperactivity Disorder) and autism. These can create difficulties with clarity and expectations of the behaviours of these children, especially if they are also on medication.

There are also the expectations that young children place on themselves and on their parents to acquire the latest gadgets and clothes. The resultant frustration often results in increased anger and defiance.

The lives that some children lead can also be very frustrating and confusing for them with a variety of dysfunctional family dynamics. It is often the young vulnerable child who is used as the 'pawn' in family squabbles. For many of these children it is perfectly understandable that they are angry with a situation they have no control over. These children have every right to feel angry and this needs to be made clear to the children. As will become a theme throughout this book, it is the way that their anger is expressed that can create even greater tensions for them in their lives. Most of these children's experiences of dealing with aggressive, negative emotions will have been based on the way their families have dealt with these emotions which is often totally aggressive. Many will not have had different role models.

From discussions with many early years staff and parents, main concerns seem to focus on the negatively viewed behaviours of defiance, aggressiveness and destructiveness.

Young children's development

At birth babies are totally dependent on their caregivers and make no distinction between themselves and their caregivers. They need to have total support from people around them. Gradually children become increasingly aware that they are independent beings and can cause things to happen around them. As children approach the age of two years they are noting what is happening around them and how other people respond to them.

A two-year-old is constantly going through a range of feelings by discovering interesting things around him – some that he can do and others that he can't or mustn't do. These young children are struggling with becoming independent beings and the responsibility that entails. With that comes confused feelings. These confused feelings result in children being contrary and can lead to quite severe temper tantrums. This is to do with wanting some clarity and some level of control over things around them. In young children these temper tantrums are usually ways of showing others that their feelings are too strong for them to manage and the children do not have the language to explain to others how they feel. Their way of telling you is by shouting and screaming, sometimes kicking and throwing things. These children are feeling angry, which is a normal feeling in the circumstances. It is important to try to understand the child's anger and respond in a sympathetic manner at the right time.

What can help?

- Understand that the child is learning how to manage feelings and will learn through imitation.

- Tell them you understand that they feel angry because they can't have the ice-cream or whatever they want right now.

- Recognise that this is an important part of growing up for the child.

- Recognise that setting clear boundaries before or immediately after an incident can provide the child with security. That doesn't mean he won't try to push the boundary but it is also part of growing up and exploring and trying to manipulate his environment.

- Use tactical ignoring where possible. If the child does not get what he wants and the adult doesn't appear to notice, the behaviour is likely to go away (eventually!).

- Let the child see that all adults feel angry at times but need to learn to manage their anger.

Ways the child may try to manage his feelings

Being clingy to adults

Some children find it difficult to become a separate person and become consequently more dependent on adults. This can also happen because the parents have a fear about their child growing up and becoming independent and the child picks up on this. Most children respond to expectations. If the expectation is that becoming 'more sensible' is valued, the child is more likely to behave like that. If adults are confused in the way that they treat the child, the child will also be confused and may show more disturbed and clingy signs of behaviour. This is almost like going back to being younger and to a time when the child felt more secure and looked after.

Fears

Young children can feel frightened over new situations and some may need more time than others to feel settled. This depends on the child's personality and some children need more attention than others to be able to join in. Some children feel 'shy' when in new situations and this is normal. Others need to be told of any likely changes.

Fads and rituals

Many children of two or three years can appear to become very fussy and will insist on things being done in a certain way that can seem obsessional.

Growing up and becoming independent is a difficult task for young children. They are now aware that they have the power to control certain aspects of the environment; when they insist on eating particular foods and wearing certain clothes they are demonstrating that they are using this knowledge.

In some cases, it's worth thinking about whether it's worth pursuing the matter and accepting the child's choice, however unusual. When occasions are dangerous clearly it will be essential that the child give in however strong the tears or tantrums may be.

There may be some occasions when these tempers are masking a child's real worry and there are real concerns and these will need to be worked at or special help sought.

Temper tantrums

Young children have strong and mixed feelings during the time of transition from baby to child. At this age the child's main communication of strong feelings is through actions. Most will not have learnt how to express their feelings verbally. Strong feelings are normal in children and gradually they need support in expressing those feelings.

Temper tantrums are a normal response to the confusion a child is feeling. When this happens a child can bite, kick, scream or do anything in attempt to dispel the overwhelming feelings he has. Most children do not scream and kick for attention. They are doing it this way because they have not learnt a more effective way of showing you how they feel. The child is probably feeling very frightened and scared of his own responses as well as feeling very angry because he feels his needs are not being met.

When this happens it is important to show the child that you can keep him safe and recognise that he is angry and upset but it will not change your decision when you say no.

If these tantrums are very powerful and continuous despite a consistent and firm approach it will be important to ask for specialist advice.

The impact on adults

Sometimes a child's tantrums can make adults feel very angry or embarrassed. Some adults can also feel they have lost any control over a child who has a temper tantrum and consequently can lose control over their ability to manage their own feelings. Adults can become as angry as the child, which will escalate the difficulty as both adult and child are attempting to control each other. This can result in a very difficult situation. Where possible adults should recognise that the child is struggling with feelings and will need support in this. Most children will learn by example and being shown how to help themselves. Initially, distraction may be helpful with young children. It is also useful for children to recognise that adults become angry and upset but they deal with it in ways other than screaming and hitting.

Who can help?

Parentline	www.parentlineplus.org.uk	0808 800 2222
Childcare link	www.childcarelink.gov.uk	0800 096 0296
Contact a Family	www.cafamily.org.uk	0808 808 3555

Children with medical difficulties

The child not the condition

The most important aspect to remember here is that the child's personality and character should be seen first and foremost and the medical difficulty second. In some cases a medical difficulty is likely to impinge on the child's personality but the way a child perceives his difficulties may be totally different from that of adults working with the child.

Children who have grown up from birth with a medical difficulty such as cerebral palsy are likely to accept their condition more readily than adults, who see the child's disability as a problem. Many of these children make good progress and become concerned mainly when adults around them show concern. Children who are diagnosed with medical conditions, such as ADHD, or have an accident at an older age may find it more difficult to adjust and may be more likely to have serious behavioural and emotional difficulties. All these children have a right to feel angry, frustrated and anxious and this should be made clear to the children.

One major aspect that is likely to be influenced by medical difficulties is the child's self-esteem. A lack of self-esteem can lead to significant behavioural and emotional difficulties. These can become increasingly difficult to manage, as it becomes tricky to isolate the child's response to his difficulty as opposed to the more usual behaviour due to other developmental factors.

A very understandable and usual situation is when parents and other adults become particularly protective over a child with medical difficulties. This situation can lead to the child increasingly feeling he cannot manage without adult support. This can lead to a highly frustrating situation for the child in which he can develop a 'learned helplessness'. In this the child loses confidence in his own abilities and becomes frustrated by his lack of the usual developmental skills. This frustration can lead to aggressiveness directed at adults close to the child when the child feels he lacks any control over his life. In these instances it will be important to recognise the child's feelings and try to discuss these with the child if appropriate.

Other difficulties can arise when the parents or carers are initially unaware of the extent of a child's difficulties. This is most likely in cases such as children with autism or ADHD. This can also result in highly aggressive behaviour due to the child's frustration.

Domestic violence

It is a sad fact that some children live in families where domestic abuse is a way of life. Even small children, while being thought to be safely upstairs in bed and 'asleep' are, nevertheless, fully aware that their parents' relationship is unhappy, imbalanced and possibly violent. It is hardly surprising that children living in this situation may arrive at pre-school tired, nervous, frightened and cautious of other people and therefore find it hard to settle into the setting.

They may be unable or unwilling to vocalise these feelings and react inappropriately in the pre-school – keeping others at a distance and reacting aggressively if others approach. Some children may present as unwilling to part from their carer who brings them to the pre-school, fearing for what may go on at home in their absence. Overheard threats the night before about 'leaving home' or 'hurting themselves' may make some children literally fight efforts to leave them at playschool for the morning, biting and kicking those who try to persuade them to enter the building and play with the other children. Others may be reluctant to go home, particularly if the abuse is directed at them, and they become anxious, spiteful and distressed as soon as people start 'clearing up' and getting coats ready to go home.

Staff need to be aware that there is a real difference between the ordinary, almost expected, 'shy' or socially unskilled child who plays up on arrival and the child who is facing on a daily basis the effects of domestic abuse in all its forms. As well as safeguarding training, which all who work with children undergo, it is advisable that staff are also encouraged to undertake domestic abuse awareness training so that they are able to react appropriately and be aware that the adults in this situation may also see the pre-school as a 'safe' place. Staff need to be prepared to be a 'listening ear' and have available the relevant literature and local contact numbers for anyone who approaches them.

Children who are hypervigilant – watchful, wary children who flinch if anyone comes too close or talks too loudly near them – children with unexplained marks on their bodies, who appear overly hungry at snack times, who react violently to others when asked to stop doing something and who never make eye contact or contribute to activities need to be monitored and careful records kept of anything that concerns the adults, ensuring that the Safeguarding Coordinator in the pre-school is alerted immediately.

Domestic abuse is not just of a physical nature; emotional abuse, including social isolation, financial abuse and neglect can also play a part in causing a child to react in a disturbing way. The pre-school setting may be the first time a child has encountered a different way of social interaction between child and adult, causing him to react in a challenging way. Children who live in a highly controlled or threatening regime at home may find the relaxed atmosphere of the pre-school difficult to cope with and even the freedom of choosing which toy to play with gives them feelings of independence that they cannot cope with. They may behave like whirlwinds of destruction as they dash from one activity to the next, testing the boundaries of the setting, or they may react the other way and refuse to play with anything other than one particular toy, aggressively fending off anyone who approaches. Children who are used to aggression in the home may frequently react violently or with verbal abuse when thwarted, thus causing upset for other children who cannot understand why their efforts at friendship are greeted with such hostility.

If a child is living in a home where domestic abuse occurs (and it must be remembered that it is not just male-to-female abuse that happens – the reverse also occurs), they may be wary of certain members of staff because they remind them of circumstances at home. Staff need to be aware that, unwittingly, they can trigger reactions that are puzzling and disturbing and if this occurs other staff need to be able to take preventative action and step in to alleviate the circumstances. Staff also need to be alert to situations when other children may say or do things which cause unexpected and sometimes violent reactions and be ready to 'divert and distract' if necessary. The provision of 'quiet' areas and 'thinking' cushions or chairs may also help give children opportunities to think things through, especially if their home is not conducive to allowing them space and time without fear of repercussions.

The key to helping children, and adults, who are coping with this situation is to provide the safest and most vigilant setting possible, to provide care and consistency, a place where everyone feels able to offload and share information and which is staffed by people who are trained and prepared to alert the appropriate agencies when necessary.

Extreme behaviours case studies

CASE STUDY 1

Violence and aggression – Aaron, three years old

Aaron was brought to the nursery by his mother after spending some 'taster days' there with her on previous occasions. She struggled up the path to the entrance while Aaron allowed himself to be 'dragged'. Once inside the entrance to the nursery, Aaron began hitting and kicking his mother. Aaron's mother offered to stay with him at the nursery but staff thought that it might be best if she left him, with an agreement to call her if he did not calm down.

Staff tried to guide Aaron into the nursery room but he continued to shout 'I don't want to' and lashed out with hands and feet. Two staff members were asked to guide Aaron into the nursery; they continued to struggle with him until he hurt a staff member with a blow to the eye area and she had to let him go. Aaron sat in the corner with his coat on and hugged his knees to his chest. He remained there for about half an hour, refusing to acknowledge staff members who approached asking if he would like to play with the cars. Staff called Aaron's mother, who collected him. Aaron could be heard shouting at his mother as he left.

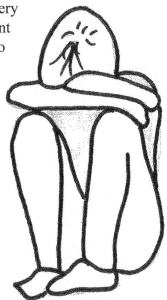

This scenario was repeated for the following two weeks. Aaron's mother decided that she would try integrating him into the nursery when he was a bit older.

Possible reasons for the behaviour

- Aaron is demonstrating genuine anger about unresolved issues.
- Aaron is using behaviours that have worked in the past in order to get what he wants.
- Aaron is following role models he has observed.
- Aaron may have poor language skills and uses behaviour to express himself.
- Aaron may be developmentally delayed and his behaviour may be an indicator of his general developmental level.
- Aaron may be on the Autistic Continuum.

Strategies

- Ask Aaron's mother to bring him to the nursery when all the other children have gone. Aaron might need to explore the unfamiliar setting in a more comfortable, secure situation with fewer unfamiliar people around. Allow Aaron to explore freely and then settle him with a favoured toy for a while until he is comfortable enough to respond to very simple interaction from an adult who works at the setting. (This may take more than one visit.) Allow mum to stay but not to guide or interact directly with him. Gradually allow mum to sit in another room and it should become clear when Aaron is ready to stay for a few minutes on his own.

- Ask Aaron's mother to bring him to the nursery when the fewest number of children are attending at first. Allow Aaron to enter the nursery only when he is calm if he resorts to hitting and shouting.

- It is important not to attempt to reason with children when they are demonstrating temper tantrums, anger etc.

- Stay calm, use a calm voice and reason with Aaron when he has calmed down.

- Be very clear about implementing firm boundaries and rules and use visual methods of conveying these. Simple line drawings are best and reduced language is vital.

- It is important to convey the message that any form of physical violence is unacceptable so swift action is necessary in order to deal with this effectively. Giving children lots of adult attention 'to explain' why violence is wrong may be misplaced especially when children are in a high state of anger. It is better to use a calm voice, reduce your language, withdraw the child to a safe place and wait until he calms down enough to understand what is being said.

- It is very important to build up a simple set of rules for children like Aaron that you expect them to be able to follow. Even if Aaron has good reasons for behaving as he does, he must learn that his method of responding is unacceptable. Aaron will learn acceptable ways of demonstrating anger in time if handled appropriately and the best time to do this is when he is very young and from the very beginning of his time at the setting.

- Since it may have taken a while (weeks) to get Aaron to stay at the nursery without hitting anyone, observations and assessments would have been ongoing. Use these to tease out what may lie behind the behaviours. Observe play skills, interaction with peers and adults, hearing and visual skills, and speech and language skills.

- Aaron's cognitive skills should be assessed when he is settled.

- A referral to a speech and language therapist and a full language assessment will help to determine his developmental level.

- If you are concerned that there may be additional difficulties and think that a paediatrician may be needed to assess Aaron, discuss this with his mother, keeping your conversation factual without adding your own opinions.
- If it turns out that Aaron is diagnosed with a specific disorder or syndrome, e.g. Autistic Spectrum Disorder, do not discount the fact that children on the Autistic Continuum are as likely as other children to be suffering from additional emotional/behavioural difficulties in parallel to autism. Language used to communicate with children on the Autistic Continuum will require modification, e.g. be unambiguous, be reduced, be accompanied by visual aids, contain instructions rather than requests.
- An individual small steps plan focused on compliance, speech and language skills, interaction, following instructions and completing adult-directed tasks could be implemented when assessments have been gathered.
- A behaviour management plan aimed at key adults could be implemented in order that all adults use consistent methods/ language to interact with Aaron and also to maintain consistently agreed sanctions.
- Referrals to other agencies will need to be considered.

CASE STUDY 2

Selective mute – Bianca, four years old

Bianca is the youngest child of three siblings, the other two being teenagers of 16 and 18. Bianca was brought to the nursery by her mother, who stayed with her for about four or five sessions and then withdrew her, reporting to staff that she 'would not settle'. Bianca rejoined the nursery when she was three years old and has attended regularly for five sessions since then. When she was first admitted, Bianca had extreme temper tantrums to the point of making herself sick. She refused to comply with simple things such as taking her coat off and changing her shoes, and responded by screaming at the top of her voice and using the phrase 'I don't want to' repeatedly. Since settling, Bianca has not spoken to any members of the nursery staff. Her mother reports that she is 'very chatty' at home and is able to use sentences to communicate. Indeed, staff report that they have observed Bianca speaking to her mother, but not in the nursery. Bianca does not interact verbally with peers and tends to stand on the periphery of their games. Occasionally, she plays more animatedly and demonstrates turn taking and laughter but does not use speech. Bianca stands still for most of the day, requiring adult prompts to engage her in an activity. Bianca has recently started giving single word answers to some direct questions, demonstrating good knowledge and understanding of basic concepts. These episodes are not consistent and Bianca can go for weeks without saying a single word to staff.

Bianca's mother has recently visited the nursery to discuss her fears that Bianca will not settle when she starts school.

Possible reasons

- Bianca has separation and anxiety issues.
- Bianca is fulfilling expectations.
- Bianca has realised that she is able to get what she wants by not speaking.
- Bianca realises that adults want her to speak.
- Bianca has a genuine fear of speaking anywhere other than in the safety and security of her home.

Strategies

- Since it is known that Bianca has good understanding of language and that there are no physical reasons for her lack of verbal communication in the nursery, staff should gather observations to assess Bianca's behaviour patterns and whether there are any reasons that she might feel unsettled or anxious.

- When Bianca is settled and leaves her mother without any separation issues, staff should agree a consistent method of handling Bianca's communication difficulties. This would necessarily involve Bianca's mother.
- Staff should continue to involve Bianca in discussions just as they would other children.
- Staff should continue to ask questions but, rather than 'demanding' a response, they should go on to the next child and then come back to Bianca briefly, to give the opportunity for her to contribute.
- If Bianca does not respond, model an answer and then move on.
- If Bianca stands in front of an adult without saying anything – adults should avoid anticipating her needs or refrain from going through a 'list' of possible needs.
- Offer Bianca a choice of two possible items whenever appropriate and model the word for her if she does not respond (she probably knows the word but is unable/refusing to say it). By modelling you are giving her the opportunity to repeat without being fearful of saying the wrong thing.
- Ask Bianca's mother to come into the setting to work on nursery tasks with Bianca.
- Extend this gradually to involving one other child and advise mum about how she should involve Bianca in communicating about the task.
- Extend further by involving a staff member and then ask mum to work at the next table.
- 'Move' mum further and further away from the place where Bianca is working with the small group until she is in the next room and then finally leaves the setting.
- Adults should not try to 'encourage' Bianca to talk or highlight the fact that she is not answering questions but rather, reduce the pressure to speak and keep the atmosphere non-threatening and non-confrontational.
- Be aware that strategies can take several months and the pace should be dictated by Bianca but definitely moved on by adults albeit in very small steps.
- A referral to the speech and language clinic is vital and, if possible, a specialist speech therapist should be involved.
- When Bianca moves on to school, this strategy may need to be repeated. Strategies should be viewed as long-term since there are usually no quick and easy remedies.
- The root cause will need to be discovered if there is to be a permanent solution but any strategies should be viewed as working over a prolonged period of time.
- Bianca's progress with the curriculum should be closely monitored.

CASE STUDY 3

Emotional disturbance – Claire, five years old

Claire has had a very difficult early life. She was given away by her teenage mother to her sister to care for. Claire's aunt did not tell her who her birth mother was and presented herself as Claire's mother. Claire's aunt has mental health issues of her own and has had two other children, one of whom died at the age of six months; the other was admitted to hospital for a non-accidental injury at the age of two years. The family are under the care of social services who have shared parental rights over the children.

Claire's birth mother recently visited the school Claire attended and announced that she was Claire's mother and that she wanted to be involved with Claire's upbringing. Claire's aunt has started to tell Claire that she no longer wants to keep her because she is 'naughty'.

Claire is very disruptive at school and demonstrates extremely limited attention and listening skills. She has sudden temper tantrums and uses foul language if adults attempt to try calming strategies. Claire does not show any interest in taking part in activities unless they are of her own choice. She lashes out at other children except for one particular child whom she never lets out of her sight. Claire insists upon playing with this child, calling her 'my best friend' even though it is not reciprocated. Claire has started to use sharp implements to attack children with. Claire likes to play with the doll's house and reproduces scenarios with the figures about death, suffocation and bleeding to death. Claire has made virtually no progress with the curriculum since beginning school.

Possible reason

* Claire is demonstrating her reactions to the emotional traumas she has endured during her life.

Strategies

- Claire is not emotionally ready to take on academic/curriculum goals and staff need to concentrate upon dealing with her primary need for security and stability.
- Staff should liaise with the family social worker closely.
- It is natural to think that children like Claire should be offered some sort of emotional counselling, individual therapy and/or family therapy. However, in a lot of authorities the reality is that these services are not available on a long-term and regular basis. It can be detrimental to give a child with obvious emotional/psychological problems irregular or therapy that is not frequent enough. It is thought that is better to start therapy when it is known that it can be frequent, regular and pitched at the correct intensity. This is a job for a professional. It would be completely inappropriate for teachers or pre-school staff to attempt to give counselling to Claire without being properly qualified.
- It is a good idea to keep a log of events about behaviours.
- Even though there are very good reasons for Claire's behaviour, firm boundaries need to be set and rules should be enforced about acceptable behaviours. Sanctions should be known and used consistently. Flexibility can be built in when Claire grows older.
- A person on the staff with pastoral responsibilities should be known to Claire and agreed exit strategies should be discussed.
- A care/management plan should be drawn up with the agreement of guardians.
- This may include strategies about a safe 'time out' space for Claire to retreat to if necessary.
- This may include strategies such as a visual timetable of the day so that a safe routine/structure can be relied upon.
- Staff should call a multi-agency meeting to plan the best way forward for Claire in school.
- Opportunities for play should be encouraged. Claire will benefit from opportunities for role play and for art and craft activities. Materials should be varied.
- Claire will benefit from opportunities to work in very small groups, with an adult who is aware of her history, on simple small steps targets focused on basic concept building. Any educational plan should have opportunities built in for repetition and consolidation.
- Claire will benefit from regular monitoring with multi-agency involvement, possibly carried out at school.

CASE STUDY 4

Physical attacks upon other children – David, five years old

David was seriously physically abused by his parents when he was a baby and toddler. He has some problems with his legs and walks with a limp as a result. David is fostered and spends time in respite care. There is a placement order upon him and he is in the process of being adopted. David has unpredictable responses to events and behaves inappropriately, e.g. laughs when children hurt themselves. David stamps on insects and worms in the gardens, pinches, pushes, scratches, hits and kicks other children. David also hides implements such as sticks and sharp metal implements in his clothes before coming to school. If undiscovered, David will use these items to attack children. David has injured other children in school and in the latest incident pushed a child's face onto the edge of a washbasin, knocking two teeth out. As the structure of the day and the curriculum have become more rigid, David has responded by increasing his aggression against peers. David responds to adults by seeming very reasonable, admitting that he has carried out these attacks, agreeing that his actions are 'not very nice' and offering no explanations at all. David's expression is neutral for most of the time. Incidents of attacks upon children are increasing and adults appear to be failing to 'get through' to David. David's cognitive and language abilities appear to be age appropriate.

Possible reason

- David is the product of a very disturbed early life and is reacting by inflicting injury/pain on peers because his emotional responses have been affected by events.

Strategies

- It should be recognised that the difficulties David is experiencing are profound in nature and that he may require lifelong therapy/interventions in order to help him to cope with what has happened to him. David has some physical injuries that are obvious. His emotional injuries are not visible but he is demonstrating the scale of these through behaviours.
- David will benefit from professional help to unravel the psychological damage and to help him to overcome these.
- In the meantime, at school, David will benefit from a completely safe and predictable routine. Key adults should draw up a care plan

for David with input and advice from his guardians and other key professionals in his life.

- The issue of physical attacks upon other children should be addressed as a matter of priority. David should be greeted every morning by a key adult with pastoral responsibilities. He should be shown his personal visual timetable and then the rules should be reinforced. The adult should not go into explanations about the rules. David should be reminded about the sanctions for any physical attacks.
- Sanctions should be used consistently but administered with care. These should be discussed with other key adults to maintain consistency.
- David should also be reminded about exit strategies used in school and that he has a 'sanctuary' if needed. David should not be 'quizzed' too closely if he needs to use the sanctuary but allowed to do something quiet such as looking at a book with an adult or on his own with an adult who is available nearby.
- David should be provided with opportunities for role play and given a safe outlet for emotions, e.g. physical play, large apparatus, painting and drawing, construction.
- David may benefit from a personal visual timetable of the day that is discussed at key points with an adult so that expected behaviours can be reinforced and also to serve as a calming influence and an opportunity to discuss any events/issues that may have arisen.
- David may benefit from a diary/liaison book and he should be encouraged to contribute to this (pictorially or with stickers) on a daily basis. He could have a choice of three faces to choose from, a smiley face, an OK face and a sad face. At the end of every session/ day there should be time set aside (a few minutes should be enough) for him to decide what kind of day it has been.
- This book should go back and forth between home and school with achievements and comments (positive) to encourage self-esteem.
- Any concerns about negative behaviours should be discussed briefly with guardians so that they are kept fully up to date with incidents and how they were dealt with.
- Incidents should be recorded.
- A regular reviewing and monitoring meeting about progress should be held more frequently than for other children and key professionals invited.
- Referral to the local child and adolescent mental health service, if not already in place, should be considered with guardians.
- David's progress should be closely monitored and transition plans for big changes (change of school) should be thought out well in advance.

CASE STUDY 5

Feeding/eating disorder – Ellen, four years old

Ellen has never been to pre-school on a regular basis and is the younger of two children, the older being 16 years old. Ellen's mother has tried to get Ellen into a pre-school, but Ellen screamed and consequently her mother stayed with her. After a few days, Ellen was withdrawn. Ellen's mother has never left Ellen with anybody else for any length of time. Ellen's mother admitted that she has 'a few problems' of her own and finds coping with life very difficult. Ellen uses mostly gestures accompanied by single words to communicate. Ellen appears to understand everything that is said to her and is able to carry out quite complex instructions. Ellen is breastfed and highlights her wish to do this by saying the word 'drink'. Ellen is not eating any solid food at all. She is under the care of a special feeding clinic and has been referred to a London hospital for a psychological assessment. A referral was made to the advisory teaching team for educational planning.

Possible reasons

- Ellen has separation and anxiety issues.
- Ellen's mother is depressed or has mental health issues that are not being addressed.
- Ellen's family have social and emotional issues that are underpinning her behaviour.
- Ellen has a physical, medical reason for an inability to take solid food.

Strategies

- Ellen's mother needs help to integrate her child into a pre-school provision.
- The pre-school should be chosen with great care and supported to admit Ellen. Ellen's mother should ask the pre-school for five morning sessions per week and aim to achieve this after a period of adjustment has taken place. Staff should expect a possible prolonged period of transition into pre-school and this should be broken down into small steps.
- Ellen should be expected to stay at the pre-school on her own after a period of supported transition agreed between parent and staff. This is likely to take a longer period than for other children.
- All key adults involved with the family should share information regularly.

- If physical or medical reasons for not taking solid food have been eliminated, the setting could begin to provide opportunities for Ellen to remain in the setting for snack/lunch times, although the idea of encouraging or even forcing Ellen to participate should be avoided at all costs. If Ellen demonstrates resistance to staying at these times, this should be reviewed with parents to discuss the way forward.
- Opportunities for playing with pretend food and 'home corner' should be provided.
- Opportunities for playing with real food should be provided.
- Opportunities for making ice lollies, biscuits, cakes, jelly etc. should be provided.
- Staff should never attempt to try to make Ellen eat anything but merely provide her with the opportunity to observe or participate in play or the making of food.
- Staff should gather observations.
- Staff should gather assessments.
- Referral to a speech and language therapist may help but consideration should be given to how many interventions the family are likely to be able to cope with at any one time.
- The health visitor attached to the family will be a vital link for drawing services together.

CASE STUDY 6

Oppositional, chaotic behaviour – Freddie, three years old

Freddie has attended his nursery for five months. He behaves entirely at random and demonstrates very high energy levels. He frequently attempts to leave the nursery room and even the school building in an attempt to get outside. Freddie has learned how to operate the security combination locks. Freddie uses the furniture like an adventure playground, jumping or allowing himself to fall from tables without attempting to break his fall. Freddie likes to play with the construction apparatus, the cars and buses. Freddie usually makes for the construction box, makes a long wheeled toy and keeps this with him for the whole session. Occasionally he holds this up to the window to look through the wheels. Freddie does not like adults to play next to him; if they attempt to engage him in an activity, he runs away. When anything formal is taking place in the nursery, e.g. when children go into small groups to do a focused activity, Freddie simply runs up and down the length of the nursery repetitively. He throws himself into the middle of the groups of children, clambering over them as though they were not there. When Freddie drops anything or accidentally knocks something over he repeats 'You naughty boy'. Freddie eats items out of the bins. Freddie does not interact with peers and demonstrates complete non-compliance with adult requests or instructions. Freddie echoes the speech of adults and demonstrates prolonged eye contact on his own terms. Freddie struggles if adults attempt to hold his hand or to guide him in any way. Towards the last part of the session, Freddie's activity levels increase; he runs up and down the nursery room, shouting, screaming at a very high pitch and banging on the windows and doors. If adults approach him, he bangs his head against the wall repeatedly.

Possible reasons

- Freddie is behaving like this because he has never experienced any form of boundary setting.
- Freddie is totally unaware of social norms and his behaviour is an indication of his developmental level.
- Freddie is demonstrating the inattention associated with Attention Deficit Hyperactivity Disorder.
- Freddie is autistic.

Strategies

- Freddie requires a highly visual method of teaching and learning and the environment will need to be easily interpreted by visual means. He will require a personal bank of visual cue cards related to his routine in the nursery. He will require sequential pictures for daily activities such as washing his hands, getting dressed etc. He will require a personal visual timetable of the session and someone to talk him through this when he comes into nursery.
- Freddie will require adults to use a visual method of communicating to accompany speech and be taught signing starting with a few main signs, e.g. 'more', to make his personal needs known.
- Freddie will probably require physical prompts/guides/handling in order to comply at first. The setting will have to review their behaviour policy and their training in this regard.
- A management plan will need to be drawn up with the advice and agreement of Freddie's parents so that issues such as physical handling can be included in management methods employed by staff.
- Physical handling should be carried out only by fully trained staff.
- Staff should concentrate upon developing compliance skills in the first instance but for very short periods, e.g. minutes, depending upon ability.
- Use Freddie's props (his wheeled toy) to encourage this, allowing him to play with it when he has complied.
- Review the routine in the nursery and consider a session of gross motor exercise at the beginning of sessions. This should be planned to include gross motor coordination, climbing, crawling, balancing, throwing, kicking and riding a tricycle.
- Freddie demonstrates a lack of a sense of danger and will need to be taught how to jump/fall safely using a safe technique. He will need to be taught when to jump from objects, e.g. during outdoor sessions when adults say you can do it.
- Use reduced, unambiguous language when speaking to Freddie. Since he uses echolalia, he may have a limited understanding of language (this will need to be assessed more fully).
- Review whether the session should be cut down for Freddie. His distress levels are raised towards the end of the session and he may be unable to cope with the high levels of stimulation in the nursery.
- Freddie should be referred to a paediatrician and to a speech and language therapist.
- The environment in the nursery may not be ideal in terms of sensory levels of stimulation and also for health and safety reasons. If

Freddie is able to escape, door locks and handles may require adaptations.

- The nursery should gather observations and assessment and consider the statutory assessment process so that Freddie's needs can be formally assessed, especially if he receives a diagnosis from a paediatrician.

CASE STUDY 7

Depression – Georgia, six years old

Georgia was the model pupil at her infant school. Georgia is a very bright, able child; she made excellent progress and enjoyed coming to school. Recently, staff have noticed that she has been very quiet and has preferred to spend time on her own rather than playing with friends at playtime. Teachers have noted a persistent tendency to be self-critical; when they praise her for good work, Georgia responds with 'it's not very good, I don't like it' or similar. Teachers and parents have noted that, whereas Georgia used to spend hours reading and working on art and craft projects enthusiastically, she now appears to have difficulty concentrating and seems tired a lot of the time. When Georgia participates in painting or drawing, she uses a lot of black or red and will often draw a picture and then cover it completely with black pencil or paint. This behaviour has lasted for longer than would be expected; there appears to be no reason for it and parents and teachers are very concerned. Georgia's mother reports that she is concerned because Georgia has lost her former good appetite and has lost weight.

Possible reasons

- Georgia is suffering from a physical illness and is demonstrating symptoms of this.
- Georgia is suffering from a mental or psychological illness.
- Georgia is reacting to events in her life/family.

Strategies

- Since Georgia's behaviour has undergone a very drastic change, adults should be concerned and begin to take action. Parents in particular and teachers need to make attempts to talk to Georgia to try to find out if there is something making Georgia feel depressed.
- Some of the more obvious things that can make children depressed are being isolated, being bullied, stress, bereavement and family breakdown.

- If there is not an obvious reason, family history may be an important contributory factor.
- The most important thing adults can do is to keep talking and asking questions. Sometimes very young children do not have the vocabulary to articulate how they are feeling, and beginning by gently asking simple questions can help. Very often, parents and teachers talk to children who are feeling sad and can think that, because the child has spoken to them about it, the problem has gone away. Children with depression often internalise their feelings and can appear to be fine to outsiders.
- Parents should plan activities that they can do with Georgia on a regular basis even if Georgia reacts with irritability. This need not be anything big but just regular time spent together to talk so that Georgia has a balance to time spent alone.
- Feeling sad and depression are very different. Depression is often characterised by the persistence of feelings of unhappiness, withdrawal, feelings of hopelessness, difficulty concentrating, tiredness, over-eating or loss of appetite and thoughts of death. These feelings do not go away.
- Research has shown that one in twelve children under 12 are suffering from depression, so the way Georgia is behaving should alert adults that they need to seek professional help.
- The local GP may refer her to the child and adolescent mental health unit.

CASE STUDY 8

Mental illness – Harry, eight years old

Harry has started to skip school. When caught by his mother, he blamed a physical illness. Harry talks about his physical health frequently and thinks that he is genuinely ill. He has also recently demonstrated a complete lack of ability to cope with ordinary daily activities, having severe temper outbursts over what his parents view as trivial matters. Harry has become very oppositional at school, defying authority and breaking rules on a frequent basis. He has been caught trying to steal items and equipment from the classroom and from other children's bags. The police have called at Harry's house when he was caught stealing from the local supermarket. Harry seems to have lost his interest in his friends and prefers to be alone for a lot of the time. Recently, Harry has been experiencing nightmares and night terrors and says that he can hear voices and that they are telling him to do bad things.

Possible reasons

- Harry is reacting to a very bad experience.
- Harry has seen something very frightening either on TV or in real life.
- Harry is suffering from a mental illness.

Strategies

- As with children who are depressed, children can also suffer from genuine mental illnesses.
- If a child is behaving much in the way described for Harry, adults should react to this with rigour.
- Harry should be referred to a specialist so that his difficulty can be treated professionally. Harry should be referred as a matter of urgency.
- Key adults in Harry's life should manage his illness with care and provide him with as secure and predictable an environment as possible.
- Key differences to look out for include inability to cope with daily activities, changes to sleeping and eating patterns, excessive complaints about physical ailments, defying authority, skipping school, stealing/damaging property, long-lasting negative moods, thoughts of death, frequent outbursts of anger, changes in performance, loss of interest in friends and family, increase in time

spent alone, excessive worry or anxiety, hyperactivity, nightmares, night terrors, persistent disobedience and aggression, frequent temper tantrums, hearing voices, hallucinations.

- For older children and teenagers, all of the above as well as drug and/or alcohol abuse, and an intense fear of gaining weight.

CASE STUDY 9

Obsessive–compulsive disorder – India, five years old

India has always had a special routine that she followed at key times of the day. It started with having to have a particular bedtime routine that included saying 'goodnight' to her dolls and teddies in a particular order. If India got the order wrong, she would have to start again. India's parents viewed this as something all young children do and they remembered that the older children in the family also had little routines they liked to stick to. As the other children grew older, these things stopped. However, as time has gone by, India has developed more and more rituals that have to be performed and the rituals have become longer and longer and more complicated and are taking up large amounts of time. When the family go out for the day, India's rituals have to be accommodated or she becomes so anxious that the day is ruined. At school, India is becoming difficult to manage because she has to perform these rituals before she is able to concentrate upon tasks and activities. India likes to order items and appears to be overly concerned with routine. She will query whether activities are safe over and over again. India refuses to become involved with anything messy and insists upon washing her hands after every session.

Possible reasons

- India is worried about something that is happening in her life and trying to maintain an element of control.
- India realises that she gets attention for these behaviours.
- India is suffering from obsessive–compulsive disorder.

Strategies

- It is known that adults affected by OCD had the condition in childhood and that this condition is sometimes ignored at that stage. It is thought that 1 per cent of children are affected.
- It is common for young children to have some minor obsessions and to like to do things such as ordering or lining up their toys. However, if obsessions and rituals are upsetting, take up a lot of time and interfere with daily life, adults should act.
- Signs to be aware of include an intense fear of dirt and germs, a fear that things are not safe, inordinate concern about order, and a fear of harming other people or doing bad things.

- Characteristic features of behaviours associated with OCD include that the actions are automatic, frequent, distressing, and difficult to control or get rid of.
- Adults should seek a referral to a paediatrician and specialist, professional help.

CASE STUDY 10

ADHD – John, five years old

John's behaviour is viewed as bizarre by staff in his infant school. He is described as 'into everything'; he shows fleeting interest but does not complete tasks or stay at anything for long. John demonstrates uninhibited behaviour, is noisy and boisterous and does not respond to the normal behaviour management techniques in place in the school. John appears not to be influenced by his peers who are providing excellent behaviour role models and seems unaware of social norms. His behaviour is often out of context and he shouts inappropriate things out or makes inappropriate noises at story times. John is always 'on the move', is restless and his behaviour appears to be without continuity or purpose. Things have become so bad at school that he is on a temporary exclusion for constant disruption and repeatedly not responding to sanctions. John is not able to access the curriculum even with a personal assistant.

Possible reasons

- John has no constraints on behaviour at home and is used to behaving on his own terms.
- John is suffering from ADHD.

Strategies

- ADHD is one of the most commonly treated conditions by health professionals.
- It seems that John is suffering at the more severe end of the continuum and adults should react to this in the first instance (when observations and assessments have been gathered) by referring John to a paediatrician.
- All key adults in John's life will need to cooperate and work closely together to plan and to action the way forward.
- John will need a high degree of structure to teaching and learning and also in his routines at home.
- John will require a differentiated curriculum and a personal education plan.
- John will need to know exactly what is expected of him with regard to behaviour and teachers should prioritise a set of prohibitions for John in order of importance: for example, aggression, lying, defiance of authority, disruption, not finishing work.

- A behaviour management plan should be drawn up with the advice and input of parents and should include agreement on rules, consequences, rewards at home and at school, key people involved, review.
- John will benefit from a personal timetable of the session/day.
- John will benefit from a timetable that is structured so that important core subjects are taught at the beginning of the day.
- John will benefit from an environment in the classroom where there is minimal movement and sensory stimulation when concentration is required.
- John will benefit from a flexible structure regarding break times, e.g. decrease in the numbers of children at play at any one time.
- John may benefit from the opportunity to wear earphones or work in a booth when appropriate in order to block out external distractions.
- Staff should provide immediate feedback on John's behaviour, use reduced language and make good eye contact when addressing him.
- Staff should 'be on hand' to provide reassurance.
- Staff should come to an agreement with John about a signal to denote 'stay on task'.
- Staff and parents need an endless supply of good humour!

CASE STUDY 11

Sexualised behaviour – Karen, five years old

Karen constantly approaches adults in her reception class and attempts to climb onto their laps. She inappropriately strokes adults whenever she gets near them, especially at story time when she presents herself at the class teacher's side. Staff have noted that her drawings are sexually explicit and that Karen uses explicit language without appearing to realise that this is not acceptable. It has also been noted that Karen approaches strangers or visitors to the class immediately and likes to sit on their laps or to cuddle them.

Possible reasons

- Karen is discovering her sexuality and does not understand where boundaries of expected behaviours are.
- Karen is reproducing behaviours learned.

Strategies

- Careful observations should be gathered; if staff are concerned that Karen may be 'acting out' behaviours she is accustomed to, i.e. that she may be being abused, they should immediately raise this with the child protection officer in the school. This is usually the head teacher or one of the senior management team members. In private nurseries or pre-schools, there should be a designated child protection officer. The issue should be raised with social services.
- This issue must be dealt with sensitively since it can be easy for adults to jump to the wrong conclusions in an effort to protect children. It must be remembered that young children do all sorts of things in imitation of television programmes, the behaviour of teenage siblings, films etc., and can 'try out' these behaviours as part of a natural growing up stage. It should also be remembered that parents should not be automatically identified or thought of as potential abusers. Abusers fall into every category of life.
- If there are good grounds for believing that this could be a case of abuse, very close liaison with social services will be vital.
- The lead should be given by the social services in this case and it may be decided to hold a multi-agency meeting in order to discuss concerns with parents. Social workers should investigate and decide upon further actions.

- At school or pre-school, staff should gently demonstrate that any inappropriate contact should be stopped. For example, if Karen tries to sit on an adult's lap, they should gently but firmly remove her and guide her to the place she should sit. They should say, 'we sit on the carpet with the other children Karen, like this'.
- Avoid negative comments, e.g. 'don't do that', 'that's not nice' etc., but highlight the appropriate, e.g. 'we sit on our own on the mat', 'we keep our hands to ourselves'.
- These interactions should be carried out in a calm tone and without emotion.
- If Karen describes a sexually explicit incident, this should be listened to without showing shock or surprise but recorded when the first opportunity arises.
- Karen is demonstrating great vulnerability when she approaches strangers so staff should highlight how to speak to visitors when they come into the room and how to react when confronted by strangers. In this respect, nothing different needs to be provided for Karen and this guidance should be a part of the typical ideas promoted by the setting. She may require much more in the way of reminders and individual guidance, however.
- Adults should model appropriate behaviours whenever possible.
- Adults should keep factual records of incidents without adding any personal opinions.
- If staff have 'suspicions' about a particular person they should never confront that person themselves but allow professional agencies to investigate.
- Staff should closely monitor Karen's progress with the curriculum to assess whether there is any impact upon learning.
- Settings should continue to provide safe, secure places for Karen to retreat to if necessary.

CASE STUDY 12

Threats to kill self – Floyd, four years old

Floyd was four years old and was due to start school soon. He had been coming into nursery for several weeks saying he was going to kill himself. He would say this to both staff and other children. After this he would just settle to an activity. Children were very reluctant to play with him as they were frightened of what he was saying and nursery staff were unsure how to deal with this.

Floyd's mother was called into the nursery and she informed staff that Floyd had stood by an open window upstairs and said he was going to throw himself out. Locks had been put on the windows and then Floyd said he would throw himself from the top of the stairs. Apart from these occasions, Floyd joined in with the normal family and nursery routine. This was a very distressing situation for both nursery and mum, who was reluctant to talk about family issues.

Possible reasons

- Floyd has experienced this type of behaviour in another person and is copying this behaviour. This may be to gain attention for himself or for the other person.
- Floyd has been very frightened by witnessing this type of behaviour, whether in real life or on television, and is acting out the situation to make sense of it.
- Floyd realises this is a way of gaining attention.

Strategies

- Most four-year-olds will have very little concept of death or suicide and this is generally a behaviour that is copied. Professional help is likely to be needed to determine where the behaviour stems from.

- Floyd could be encouraged to discuss issues of concern to him through artwork or other creative means.
- Floyd will need constant reassurance to let him know that he can talk to any of the adults if there is anything at all that is worrying him.
- Floyd may be severely lacking in self-esteem, and may need a high level of very positive support. He should be encouraged to talk about good things he has done at nursery or at home.
- Floyd may have recognised that he gains attention by making such comments. If there are not obvious reasons found for this behaviour it should be ignored where possible and a focus should be given to all positive aspects of Floyd's actions.
- Staff should discuss these difficulties with both parents if this is possible. This could prove difficult where there are highly emotive family issues. Some parents discuss inappropriate things in the presence of young children. It is possible that Floyd has heard something and is trying to make sense of the situation and is very frightened of it.

Outcome

After several more weeks of this behaviour, Floyd's parents did access specialist family support. Reluctantly Floyd's father did attend the sessions as concerns for Floyd were growing stronger. During the course of the sessions it emerged that Floyd's father had periods of significant depression and had lost several jobs through this. He had attempted suicide on several occasions and had been admitted to hospital several times. Floyd had witnessed this behaviour.

When these issues emerged, nursery staff were able to recognise Floyd's cry for help at living within a strained family environment and were able to understand his difficulty. They were advised to allow him to express his feelings where possible. Once Floyd realised that staff understood his position he was able to talk more openly on occasions. Gradually, Floyd spoke less about killing himself and more about how he could help his dad be more happy.

CASE STUDY 13

Self-harm – Zachary, nearly three years old

Zachary is nearly three and has been attending pre-school for about six months. Until recently he has been 'quietly content' in the setting, socialising with a couple of children on a regular basis but also playing with different children when the opportunities occur. He has an elder brother who started in mainstream school a year ago and there is a new baby girl in the household. He usually parts happily from his mother or grandmother who sometimes brings him to school.

He arrived at school a few weeks ago with a red mark on his forehead, which his mother said he had done while playing in his bedroom on the carpet with his cars. Although this mark has not healed up well, Zachary has not mentioned it or complained about his head being sore. Yesterday a member of staff found Zachary in the book corner on his own, banging his head hard against the floor. When she asked him to stop he burst into tears but quietened down when she offered to read him a story. Later on a different member of staff found him in the cloakroom area with another child who was watching open-mouthed as Zachary struck his forehead hard on the edge of the sink. She stopped him from doing any damage and gave him a cuddle. When his mother arrived to take him home at the end of the session she was told about the incident. She was in a hurry but agreed to talk to Zachary about it, saying that she would put some cream on the now very red and sore-looking place.

Any form of self-harming is very disturbing for adults and children to witness and instances need to be addressed as soon as possible. With some children who are old enough to have acquired good language skills or who find it hard to express themselves verbally, it can be a sign that they need attention and have learnt that by making an overt gesture that gets a reaction from others they can gain a lot of attention very quickly. Zachary may well be feeling that, with his brother now in full-time school and a new baby in the house, his needs are not being given the priority they once were and has found a sure-fire way of getting some attention. For some children the pain they cause themselves is not the main issue and they repeat their actions because they become used to the attention and care they get as a consequence. Some children would far rather have negative or angry responses than no attention at all and it is vital that the self-harm is not allowed to escalate. For staff in the pre-school it is important that they log any incidents of self-harm and discuss them with the parents/carers immediately. By keeping a vigilant eye open for opportunities when Zachary could begin to bang his head and by giving him some extra time and attention, the pre-school will probably be able to reduce the likelihood of his self-harming during his sessions. As his habit of head banging apparently started in his home, regular liaison with his mother and grandmother is essential to encourage them to keep a very watchful eye on him, and if necessary, encourage them to seek help from other agencies such as their GP, Health Visitor or local Children's Centre if the problem persists.

SECTION 3

Anger management

Introduction

All emotions are a normal part of human development. These emotions alert us to how we are interacting with others and with our environment and help to develop mature thinking and acting. But learning to understand emotions can be a difficult part of growing up. From birth most emotions are spontaneous and adults can generally understand the emotion through watching the baby or the child's body language. A smile or excitedly moving the hands suggests a happy child and most positive emotions are easy to respond to. Difficulties can arise when actions associated with healthy expression of more negative emotions by a young child are seen as naughty or aggressive and the child is not taught more appropriate ways of responding.

The most frightening emotion for a young child to understand and to express in a socially acceptable way is anger. This can be equally difficult for the adults who are with the child at the time. One main reason for this is that in our society the expression of anger is generally viewed as a negative act. The idea still exists that the expression of emotion should not be seen in public as much emotion is considered to be aggressive and destructive. This is particularly so with the emotion of anger.

The reality is that anger can be a very useful indicator of how the child is managing situations around him and the expression of anger should be encouraged. The key to this is to teach the child how to express his anger in a socially acceptable way. All children should be made aware that it is perfectly normal to feel angry and that everybody feels angry at times. Parents or adults working with children have the perfect opportunity to constantly model socially acceptable ways of demonstrating anger. This can be made clear to children by telling them that you feel angry about something specific – maybe the way they have been acting – and then how to deal with this. This could be by saying something like 'You'll need to sit alone for a few moments to think about what to do next.'

A major difficulty about the emotion of anger is that the feelings associated with anger can escalate very quickly and these feelings can spread to other people around. One way of thinking about this is by picturing the anger as a red hot ball of fire. When the child feels angry this ball of fire gets hotter and the child wants to get rid of it by throwing it at other people. Adults or other children around may catch this fire but it also may become too hot for them to hold so they throw it back. Several people can become heated by the anger, which can continue to grow and engulf most people present. This can prove a highly frightening experience. A further way of thinking about anger is through an Anger Mountain staged diagram, which will be explained later in this chapter.

The most dangerous, frightening and destructive aspect of anger is the way some children's anger escalates so rapidly that they appear to be totally out of control of this emotion. Imagine our ball of fire as having progressed to totally engulfing the child so that they can no longer see, hear or feel what is happening around them. All they can do is to try and get rid of this ball by kicking, screaming, hitting out or throwing things around. In my work with young children several have expressed these feelings when they have calmed down and are able to discuss things more rationally. Several children have said that it feels 'really hot' when they are angry and one child said he had to splash his face and hands in cold water to try to cool down.

A child who is engulfed in anger is not rational. This is not the time to talk to the child; wait until the anger has subsided.

In the *Oxford English Dictionary*, anger is defined as 'extreme displeasure' and described as an 'instinctive feeling as opposed to reason'.

This negative view can be very unhelpful when trying to support young children. A more useful way is to think of anger in the following ways:

- as a secondary emotion that may arise from a primary emotion such as fear. It is bound up with embarrassment, injury, disappointment, exploitation, envy and loss. All these represent a threat of some kind;
- as a reflection of emotional difficulties;
- as a behaviour which achieves particular outcomes and is maintained.

Anger is always a reaction to something. This can be real or perceived and shows us that something is wrong.

There are three basic types of anger:

- a response to frustration when our needs are not being met;

- a calculating way to get an end result;

- the release of pent-up emotions particularly when the child feels powerless to effect change and is at the end of his emotional tether.

Problem anger can achieve short-term goals, such as being able to stay up later by means of crying, but it is always at the cost of long-term solutions. Children should be taught to express anger in a socially acceptable way.

Dealing with an angry child

When faced with an angry child it can be very useful to be really clear about how both the child and you respond. The following Observation Sheet may prove helpful in identifying patterns of behaviour and planning support for the child.

OBSERVATION SHEET

1. What was the situation that made the child angry?

2. Where and when did this happen?

3. How exactly did the child behave?

4. What did the child say that made you feel he was angry?

5. What did the child do that made you feel he was angry?

6. How strong would you rate the child's anger?

    a. Irritated

    b. Annoyed

    c. Cross

    d. Angry

    e. Extremely angry

7. How did the child show his anger?

    a. Non-verbally – facial expression, posture etc.

    b. Verbally – shouting, swearing

    c. Physically – hitting, kicking

    d. Leaving the situation

8. Whom or what did the child appear to be angry with?

    a. Mainly himself

    b. Mainly other people

    c. Mainly an object

    d. Things in general

9. What did you do?

10. How did the child respond?

From Angela Glenn, Alicia Helps and Jacquie Cousins, *Managing Extreme Behaviours in the Early Years*, London: Routledge © 2009 Angela Glenn, Alicia Helps and Jacquie Cousins

It is useful to consider the purpose that anger serves; it has many positive as well as negative functions. The following summary may help you to become more aware of the functions of anger.

DYNAMICS OF ANGER

- Demands attention
- Can lead to aggressive or depressive behaviour
- Panic response indicating that those who become angry believe themselves rightly or wrongly to be in danger
- Once the anger becomes the dominating emotional response it leads children to behave in ways that perpetuate it

Anger released through aggressive behaviour leads to rejection or to others behaving aggressively in return. Both responses cause more anger, creating a vicious circle.

NEGATIVE EFFECTS OF ANGER

- It prevents rational thinking
- It results in harmful behaviour
- It results in withdrawal/isolation/rejection
- It blocks other feelings
- It prevents self-awareness and change
- It can be addictive

POSITIVE EFFECTS OF ANGER

- It provides energy for action
- It expresses tension or conflict
- It is a sign of a problem or problems
- It can motivate change
- It warns others of your limits
- It gives self-protection

When dealing with an angry child the main aims should always be to limit the damage the child can do to himself or to others and to help him calm down and regain some control of his emotions.

Here are some do's and don'ts:

DO

- Where possible avoid audiences. Move other children away to a different area of the room or a different room if possible. In many cases it will be difficult to move the angry child.

- Remain very calm and talk in a very slow manner and use very simple language.

- Assure the child you understand he feels very angry and that you can help him.

- Encourage the child to talk, and listen to the child.

- Always offer a 'way out' or choice, e.g. 'would you like to sit quietly in the book area and let me know when you are ready to come back?'

- Tackle the matter later, preferably after you have managed to think about the situation and filled out an observation sheet.

- Return to normal as soon as possible.

- Explain to the child that it is normal to feel angry in certain situations.

DON'T

- Don't over-question the child by asking why he acted that way. The aim is to calm the child.

- Don't be threatening or negative.

- Don't go for a win–lose outcome. The aim is to help the child recognise his own feelings and responses and manage them more effectively.

- Don't intrude on the child's personal space where at all possible. Talk to the child from a short distance away.

An Anger Mountain is a useful way of thinking about the five stages involved in an angry outburst.

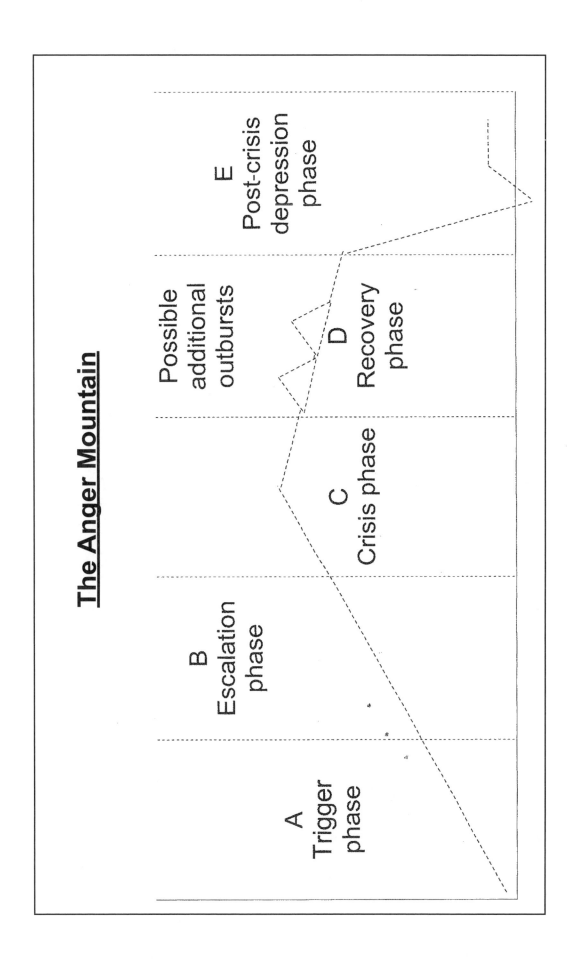

The Anger Mountain

A
Trigger phase

B
Escalation phase

C
Crisis phase

D
Recovery phase

Possible additional outbursts

E
Post-crisis depression phase

Stage A

At the trigger stage try to divert the child if possible. The aim is to help the child identify the warnings or indicators of anger for himself. For many children these can be physical. The adults may notice that the child clenches his fists, goes red in the face or the body tightens and shoulders are stiff and brought together. It is helpful if the child and adults can become aware of these physical indicators and have a plan of action or can ask an adult for help.

Another useful technique may be to use tension releasers with children who are regularly angry. Suggestions could be, if space permits, allowing the child to run around for a short while at intervals or use quiet soothing music as a background to some activities. In some early years settings adults use a two- to three-minute burst of activity lessons in which a small group of children have an 'exercise time' each hour to allow children to use up energy in a constructive way.

Stage B

This stage will see a rise in behaviour and emotion. It is still possible to bring the child back at this stage by giving him a 'calming place' to go to. The aim at this stage is to keep the child as calm as possible to avoid further escalation.

Stage C

At this stage the child has 'lost it' and is no longer able to reason or listen. The aim here is damage limitation and keeping the child and others around him secure. Some children have described being in this stage as being unable to hear or feel anything. Many young children become so engulfed by the anger that they have no control over the situation, which can be very frightening for them as well as onlookers.

Stage D

After a peak has been reached the only way is down. The child gradually begins to slow down physically and emotionally. As the child is still emotionally charged there can be further outbursts at this stage. If possible encourage the child to move to a quiet area and keep other children away. Adults should still keep a short distance away and use a calm, reassuring voice and manner.

Stage E

Following the angry outburst, there is a sudden drop in physical and emotional energy. As a result of the abrupt drop in hormone level this often leads to a depression phase in which the child is in tears or finds it difficult to move. This stage can last up to several hours. This is not the time to discuss the events with the child.

After any angry outburst there needs to be a time of reflection for child and adult together to discuss the situation and how things could be changed. This may need to happen the following day if the child has a short pre-school session.

The following ideas may prove helpful:

BEFORE

- Stay calm.

- Acknowledge the child's feelings.

- Ask the child what would help him feel better about the situation.

- Use a calming place and some time away.

- Divert the child's attention.

- Use tension releasers such as running around, relaxation techniques or soothing background music.

DURING

- Allow the child his 'space'.

- Keep at the child's eye level if talking to him and speak in a calm manner.

- Try not to make direct eye contact.

- Use a very slow, calm voice and very simple language.

- Have a plan ready such as moving other children away if possible.

AFTER

- Return to normal as soon as possible.

- Use an observation sheet to look for patterns.

- Encourage the child to join in with a discussion on how to change these situations.

- Keep looking for new ideas.

- Reassure the child that feeling angry is normal but he needs to show his anger in a different way.

- If damage has been done, decide on ways to make amends.

- Constantly reassure the child you are trying to help him and want to understand him better.

CASE STUDY 14

Supporting an angry child – Joachim, four years old

Joachim was the youngest of four children. His 14-year-old brother had been in trouble with the police and had problems at school with bullying so his mum had kept him off school. His other two siblings seemed average in most ways.

Joachim would often be brought into nursery kicking and screaming at his mother and then he transferred his kicking and screaming to nursery staff. This resulted in staff being bruised and reluctant to be involved in the handover. After about 10 to 15 minutes Joachim would settle down to an activity and play well on his own. He did not relate well to the other children and insisted on playing with specific toys on his own. When other children came to play with the equipment he would often lash out at them. Consequently children were very wary of him and mainly kept away.

It was decided to try to involve Joachim in sessions about managing his own behaviour as he appeared a capable boy whose language and cognitive skills seemed to fall into the average range. Joachim's mother seemed at her wit's end with dealing with him and commented that he was constantly aggressive at home. It was felt that the initial focus would be on a change in the nursery sessions.

In this case five separate sessions of about 10 to 12 minutes were used with the Special Needs Co-ordinator of the nursery, who had been advised of this programme by the Education Psychologist. Each strategy taught would be carried out and practised over a two-week period or more if necessary. Joachim's mother was made aware of the plan and was asked to support the system at home if she was able to.

Session 1

Through the use of pictures Joachim was asked to try to recall his personal physical responses when the other children approached him in the nursery. Joachim was able to say that he noticed that his head became 'stuck' and his teeth came together and he put whatever he was holding next to him so that nobody could take it. Joachim was able to say that his hands felt sticky.

In this session Joachim was put into a role play situation in which the adult pretended to be the other child and Joachim was taught to keep his hands open and by his side. During the session Joachim was able to tell the adult that he enjoyed sitting on his beanbag at home and watching the television. He was asked to bring in some photographs from home of him sitting on his beanbag. His keyworker would try to keep a watch out where he was playing and put the photo so he could see it where possible. He was also advised to keep a small photograph in his pocket and to think of himself sitting on the beanbag when another child came near him.

He was asked to try to remember other things he noticed as well during the next few days.

Session 2

This session focused on what made Joachim angry and identifying:

- incidents, however trivial they might seem;
- physiological responses as discussed in previous session;
- thoughts at the time.

This session continued with supporting Joachim and trying to help him to understand his own anger and trying to become aware of what could be causing it. This session would continue with role play situations and helping Joachim to recognise his own feelings. In these cases it is very useful to help the child to think about his thoughts and how he could change those thoughts. For example, Joachim said that he felt really hot when he thought another child wanted to play with the same toy that he had. He noticed that he held it really close to him and his hands and shoulders became very tight as if he were 'in a pipe'. Joachim was able to say that he didn't want to share the toy and in his head he was saying 'If he comes near me I'm gonna really go for him and kick him out of sight.'

In this session Joachim was asked to think about sitting on his beanbag at home when another child came near him and to say to the child 'I'm playing with this at the moment but you can have it later.' Joachim was told to talk to his keyworker whenever he managed to think like this. His keyworker kept a lookout for any potential situations so that she could support Joachim where possible.

Session 3

In this session Joachim was asked how things were working. This session focused on thinking of possible alternative responses to the situations Joachim found difficult. This was also done through role play.

This part of the process continued for four weeks before moving onto the next stage. Each time a problem situation occurred Joachim was aked to act out more appropriate strategies once he had calmed down.

This part would also involve the other child or children in question when possible so that several different role play strategies could be tried out. This process proved very successful for the pre-school and they have carried on using this strategy for other children. The children together then could discuss how they felt with the different approaches.

Sessions 4 and 5

These sessions focused on Joachim's thinking and he was asked to use different words to himself when he felt that he was 'losing it'. When he felt the stiffening in his hands or neck he was asked to say things to himself such as 'keep calm', 'breathe slowly', 'count to five: one – two – three – four – five', 'cool it', 'deep breath'. He was also advised to walk away whenever he was able to and go to a given calming area.

Session 6

If he managed to keep his anger under control he would continue to talk to himself. 'You did good there', 'That was OK', 'Move away, it's not worth the hassle', 'Forget it'.

Joachim was asked to become consciously aware of what he was thinking. If he wanted to he could tell his keyworker and she would write it down or he could record it on a tape.

Nursery support

Nursery was asked to provide a place of safety – 'a calming corner' – that Joachim could go to or be sent to if he or staff noticed that he was ready to 'kick off'. Joachim's keyworker was given time to record Joachim's responses, and support him in moving to the calming area if it looked as if he needed it. She was also asked to complete an observation sheet.

Outcome and evaluation

Evaluations are from Joachim and the staff. When Joachim was asked what he thought, he said he thought it was 'weird' to think about what he was thinking and he found it hard but staff had helped him by saying the calming words that he liked and he liked to have somewhere to go to to move away with his toy.

The most helpful aspect was that Joachim did slowly improve with his hitting out and kicking at nursery and by the end of the year had made one good friend that he could share toys with. Other children also started to approach Joachim and ask to play with him. Joachim's mum had also noticed an improvement at home and he no longer screamed and hit out getting to the nursery.

The core principle is that anger management is a compilation of stress reduction techniques for channelling angry feelings into socially acceptable directions. Any anger management programme will be a combination of relaxation and specific interventions.

SECTION 4

Promoting positive behaviour

Introduction

Lifestyle choices that influence children's behaviour

Nurture groups

The Boxall profile

Introduction

Pre-school settings are usually the first opportunity that many children have for finding out about the society they belong to. With many children growing up in relative isolation from wider family networks or living in flats with little opportunity to play outside, the pre-school premises with its associated noise and bustle and range of play activities on offer can have a profound effect on children. It is up to the adults in any education setting to ensure that they demonstrate high standards of appropriate interaction among themselves as well as with the children and their families.

Of course it is helpful if the setting itself has the obvious 'positive' signs – things such as a welcoming entrance, neatly produced signage, well displayed notices and professionally produced literature all play their part in creating an efficient and positive image. Most establishments have copies of the 'Golden Rules' prominently displayed and children's pegs and boxes neatly labelled. However, an attractive setting, although it can help, does not necessarily ensure that an ethos of positive behaviour is in place. Every opportunity needs to be taken to encourage children and parents/carers to see education as a positive experience. How the children and their families are met and greeted on arrival every day can make a real difference in how education is perceived. Some parents have very rosy views on their schooldays and encourage their children to see school in an equally positive light, but there are others for whom school was a miserable and daunting time. In order for all children to feel included it is vital that the 'whole package' is seen as a place where all the family is welcome. Children in the early years may not be able to understand all that is *said* to them but they are very good at picking up the body language and tone of the adults around them and first impressions are often highly significant.

Those who work in early years settings need to be vigilant in all their dealings with others and care needs to be taken that politeness, respect for personal space and facial expression are carefully monitored. Children who are difficult to manage frequently have poor skills in interpreting social cues; if the adults in the setting are ambiguous, express personal comments (even in a humorous way) or use negative body language this can make the child wary and suspicious that they or their carer are not welcome. Without the necessary language skills to express their anxiety or negative feelings about spending time in the establishment, some children quickly resort to aggression or resistance and begin to get a 'reputation' for poor behaviour. This frequently occurs in the fairly public arena of the reception area and all too easily the impression is given of a child who is going to be 'trouble'.

Some pre-schools have managed to alleviate the problem of on-arrival flare-ups by deploying a sympathetic adult whose job at the start of every session is to meet and greet each child and, if necessary, direct them to a quieter area to sit and cuddle a toy or look at a book with their carer until the adult has a chance to talk them through the routine of the day, what toys and activities are available that day and any changes to the usual routine that are happening that day. Children who are inarticulate verbally may often have observational skills that are not always appreciated. It is not unknown for a small child to notice that, for instance, the car belonging to the Pre-school Supervisor is not in the car park. Without having the skills to ask questions, they may fear that the usual routine is going to change or be disrupted in some way; before the day has started their anxiety levels are raised and they are unable to cope. By arranging to have another adult explain, gently and when they are ready, that everything is normal, much can be done to keep behaviour cool, calm and collected. If the building does not lend itself to providing a quiet area, some schools have bought a small, collapsible igloo-type tent which children can sit in while they let themselves calm down and wait for the majority of the children to enter the school. This can be a very effective way of letting the child hear what is going on while he gathers his thoughts. Other schools arrange for children who have problems parting from their carer to arrive slightly earlier or later than the others so they miss the hurly burly of the cloakroom area (and the parent is also able to avoid the sometimes disapproving or smug expressions of other parents!).

Other schools are good at pre-empting possible problems by making sure that everyone has adequate warning of events coming up. Sending letters home to inform the families of visits by entertainers or the photographer is an essential way of communicating information, but some establishments have found it helpful to use simple, old-style chalkboards and easels with handwritten notices displayed outside on the approach to the building to re-publicise the information. This also helps to alert parents and carers who are not as literate as others and who discard formal communications rather than admit they cannot read all of the letters. There is a real need for verbal dissemination of information; a lot of unnecessary disquiet can be saved by organising one of the staff to be in the reception area at the end of the day to remind people collecting their children that the next day is when the juggler is coming or give reminders that the establishment is closed for the Bank Holiday etc. If the establishment is in an area where there is a large ethnic mix, having speakers of relevant languages available to assist and ensuring that written communication is translated can help to defuse tensions and promote inclusion for all.

Better training has ensured that educational establishments these days are staffed with people who know how to talk to children and have a good understanding of child development. However, one area in which training is not easily available is how adult-to-adult communication is carried out. It is not unknown for individuals to talk to the children in their care in a positive and encouraging manner but address their co-workers in a peremptory or even critical way. Words are not the only way of communicating and the tone in which it is done and the accompanying body language can say things which words cannot convey. Children are often adept at interpreting what is going on, particularly if they live in households where tension and sudden aggression are signalled by looks and gestures, and they can quickly become aware if there is friction between members of staff. Some children will exploit this for their own ends, having had lots of practice at manipulating adults at home. Others, sensing that all is not well, will lose concentration, become anxious, take avoiding action and refuse to comply or simply become upset and intractable. Others may just become aggressive and hit out at others or throw objects around. If this happens it is all too easy for the adults to escalate the situation by raising their voices, getting closer to the child or physically trying to stop him. In the first instance it may be worth trying to de-escalate matters by giving the child some space, removing any other children from the immediate area and keeping verbal requests to an absolute minimum. When a child is so angry or frustrated that he is hurling things around he is unlikely to be listening; questions such as 'why are you doing . . .' and comments such as 'That's a silly way to behave – you won't be able to go out to play now' are highly unlikely to result in the child ceasing his actions.

When staff feel they are working well together and the children are responding appropriately it is very easy to sound and behave in a positive, up-beat way. Attractive surroundings, a full complement of trained staff and a range of good quality equipment all help to encourage everyone to respond in a positive and encouraging way to even quite challenging behaviour. However, if circumstances change – a key employee rings in sick or bad weather threatens a planned outdoor activity – it can be only too easy for staff to feel inadequate or stressed, and negative feelings and comments begin to creep into the day. Children often respond in a similar fashion and those whose emotions are very near the surface can begin to play up or behave aggressively, demanding attention from all and sundry.

It is at times like this when investment in relevant training and having clear lines of responsibility really do help to keep the whole setting on an even keel. A well organised setting needs to have clear guidelines for staff, with areas of responsibility set out with tasks allocated fairly so that when circumstances alter it is easy to reallocate duties in a straightforward way. Staff knowing what each other does and having experience in all aspects of the setting will make for a cooperative and well managed establishment.

All education settings need to have a behaviour policy and list of strategies to be employed that are readily available for all staff to read and take heed of.

Regular meetings need to be set up to discuss individual pupils and time needs to be put aside for these discussions to take place well away from the hearing of any pupils. Remarks such as 'Oh, we always leave him well alone when he is in one of these moods. He's always like this just before playtime' will just serve to reinforce unwanted behaviour and signal to others that the child is someone to be wary of. Clear and concise policies and guidelines are essential for all establishments and these need to be revisited by all the staff and issues discussed so that everyone is clear about procedures.

All staff must be trained in safeguarding (child protection) and first aid training is also a must but it is also advisable for staff to have attended training opportunities in a wide range of activities – child development, speech and language, play skills and play leadership, Signalong or Makaton. Staff who feel skilled and competent in their jobs will have the confidence to deal with challenging situations.

If a child really becomes uncontrollable, staff need to work together to restore everyone's equilibrium. Moving the child to a quiet area, removing items that can be thrown and cause damage, providing a big soft cushion or beanbag for the child to pummel or lie down on when he has exhausted himself and, most importantly, removing an audience can all help to speed up the calming-down process. If a child has 'lost it' big time, careful notes should be made of the incident, including the time of the day, the trigger for the behaviour (if known), who was present, what action as taken at the time and notes for follow-up action. An example of a simple recording sheet is included at the end of this chapter. If a child has had a major tantrum once, it may be that it will happen again and a plan needs to be drawn up so that everyone knows what to do in the future. Quite often a child has a major tantrum once and never repeats it, but others can almost get into a habit of causing mayhem, and by keeping detailed records staff can start to pinpoint the triggers or time of the day and make plans to minimise the risk of repetition.

Some settings find it helpful, with a 'repeat offender', to make a simple weekly recording chart, noting the child's behaviour on a scale every quarter or half hour. A scale of 1 (being happy and on task) through to 5 (off task and physically aggressive) can be a very useful way of identifying the pattern of behaviour. A copy of such a chart is included at the end of this chapter. By keeping a chart such as this for a couple of weeks or so it may be possible to pinpoint a time of the day or particular activity as an especially sensitive time and steps can be taken to alter the child's routine to try and avoid or minimise the number of incidents. Parents and carers need to be kept fully informed if their child is the subject of such intensive record keeping. In fact some settings have found that the families welcome such care and interest in their offspring and wish to keep a similar chart for behaviour at home. Children who regularly throw major tantrums in an education setting are often just as volatile at home, although because most families have a less timetabled regime than a school the triggers may be less obvious. Families often banish the tantrum-thrower to his bedroom whereas in an education setting it is not so easy as there may not be any safe spare space to use.

Recovery time is also important – for the child and any adults who were involved. It is distressing to witness a child who is beside himself with rage or frustration and any adult who has been kicked, bitten or spat upon needs some recuperation time too. Having a staff debriefing session at the end of the day and careful handover meetings can go a long way to restore confidence and is a good way of ensuring consistency between members of staff. Quite unwittingly, a team member can trigger an unwanted behaviour just by accident if she is not fully aware of the plan for a particular child. The child concerned needs to feel the next day is a new day but staff also need to feel that their concerns have been discussed. No one should be going home with negative feelings because matters have not been discussed fully.

The effectiveness of the establishment lies with the competence and attitude of the people in it – a smile from an adult can go a long way to helping a troubled child begin to trust adults. Consistency and patience are not always easy but if staff are able to treat each other in a positive and caring way the children will notice this and learn that education is a safe and happy part of their lives.

Lifestyle choices that influence children's behaviour

All families are different and it is important to allow individual freedom and diversity to flourish. However, when children enter the world of education there is frequently an expectation that, for certain parts of the day, a greater degree of conformity and a specific standard of behaviour are necessary in order to allow the functioning of the setting to be safe and organised. Family life is the most important factor in a child's development but may conflict with the more structured approach most educational settings use.

One of the most common influences in the home is the television and media generally and because it is so usual for homes to have a television on throughout the day it is easy to 'forget' it is there. Now that portable DVD players (complete with earphones) fitted in cars are also very common, skills such as looking out of the car window and commenting on the scenery, playing 'I Spy' or counting the number of red front doors passed during the journey, and taking the opportunity for conversation (or even the chance of learning to cope with boredom!) are less likely to be encouraged.

Over the past decade it has become almost the 'norm' for even very young children to have bedrooms that have the sort of gadgetry which almost duplicates what was previously found only in the living room. Televisions, DVD players and computer games seem to be standard issue and if children share bedrooms with older siblings then the list expands to an amazing degree. Although it is true that most children have no problems telling fact from fiction, or understanding that what they have seen on television is just a programme, others often have access to programmes or DVDs which are totally inappropriate for the early years. With the advent of huge television screens in the living room it is now quite common for babies and toddlers to be surrounded by their own toy things in a room where the TV is dominant over all other forms of communication.

It has been said that televisions are used as babysitters – to keep even tiny babies 'entertained' whilst parents get on with cooking meals, washing clothes or talking on the telephone. There can't be many parents who have not resorted to a quick 'fix' of the Teletubbies while they nip to the loo or answer the front door. However, there is a world of difference between this quick and expedient use of the television and leaving babies parked in front of the box for large parts of the day. With the wide availability of Sky and Freeview channels there are many programmes available during the day which are a poor substitute for personal interaction with parents/carers and other members of the family. Much of what a toddler acquires in language skills has little to do with the actual words spoken – facial expression, body language, tone and speed of delivery of the spoken word are vital experiences and allow children to master the complex skill of communication. Regrettably, a lot of what is seen on the television provides a very unreal experience. Just try watching an early evening 'soap' or a daytime 'reality' show with the sound turned off and study the facial expressions and frequently aggressive body language demonstrated and you will begin to see that today's youngsters are exposed to an extremely confrontational style of communication.

Try counting in seconds the camera hold time during programmes and you will see that five seconds is about the maximum length of time the camera angle is held before it shifts, or that the camera shows one actor while the dialogue is being spoken by another character off screen. It will become clear why some children have great difficulty listening to others, following instructions and concentrating on any activity in the pre-school setting. Story or carpet time, with one adult sharing a book with a group of children, can be a difficult time for many children who are unused to participating in such a static, single-adult-led activity. Of course, many children soon settle into the pattern of listening to stories and rhymes and enjoy having simple visual prompts clearly presented, but there will always be some who are so firmly 'hooked' on a channel-hopping/remote control style of entertainment that they disrupt or ignore this essential part of the education process, finding following action rhymes or joining in singing activities with others too hard.

When talking to parents who are concerned about their child's progress in the pre-school or who are worried that his speech seems limited in comparison with others, it might be worth discussing how their arrangements at home may or may not be having an impact. There is no substitute for the bedtime routine of bath, followed by a short story read while the child snuggles down in bed. Many, even tiny, children are now settled down for the night with their favourite cartoon on a TV in their bedroom. If used as a treat this can give the parents some very valuable time but the bright colours, loud sound effects and often rapid-fire speech patterns of many of the characters are not the best thing to get children off to a sound night's sleep. If the parents do not seem inclined to do the bedtime story bit, it might be worth suggesting to them that a story or nursery rhyme tape, played quietly with no visual stimulation, may be a better way of getting their child off to sleep and also encourage the development of listening skills which will help them in the pre-school setting.

When staff talk to parents about a child who appears tired in the school setting, the parents invariably say that their children are always in bed 'nice and early' and 'we always turn their TV off'. Today's toddlers are more than capable of using a remote control and parents are kidding themselves if they think their child hasn't worked out how use it and turn the sound down. Sleep deprivation and late nights are bad for all of us and children starting out on their education need to be fully rested and ready for a busy morning in the nursery if they are to benefit from all that a good pre-school setting can provide.

Some families lead very busy lives and will find it nigh on impossible to keep to a strict bedtime story routine every night of the week, but raising the importance of the need for small children to hear the sound of a real human voice reading a simple story to them at the end of the day may encourage them to at least increase the number of times they try and fit one in.

Computer games and electronic toys cannot be ignored – it takes a very determined parent not to succumb to pleas for the latest 'must have' toy. One only has to watch television at the weekends to see the amount of advertising aimed at children and it is no surprise that even the most unworldly youngsters know what is available in the shops. However, many children would, given a choice, rather spend twenty minutes playing Snap or picture dominoes with a carer than spend a similar amount of time playing a matching game on a computer screen. With 'real' people the skills of turn taking, watching others take their time, using manipulative skills to turn cards and place dominoes or counters, and learning to cope with the success of winning and the feeling of disappointment of losing a game are essential skills for success in coping with educational settings and interaction with peers. Children may well develop a high level of skill in picture matching and visual discrimination with the aid of a computer game but if you are not 'winning' it is all too easy just to hit the escape button and start again, and again, and again. This is very poor preparation for learning to play with other children.

Many of the old-fashioned games and activities (pushing cars, threading beads, block building, dressing dolls and teddies, moving counters etc.) require hand-to-eye coordination and using a tripod grip, which are vital pre-writing skills. Many children, when they start pre-school, become frustrated and angry that they cannot do some of the activities on offer because they do not have the necessary dexterity to pour water or do a jigsaw and give up at the first attempt or expect someone to do it for them. So many modern toys and games require primarily the use of thumbs to operate the remote control or keypad that, if children are not given the opportunity to develop a range of hand muscles, they will be at a serious disadvantage when presented with crayons and paintbrushes in school. Frustration with being unable to make satisfactory marks on paper can result in tantrums, lashing out at others and tearing up paper, which will upset others and begin to set the pattern for early failure in attempting new activities. This is characteristic of children whose parents are asked to 'pick them up early' or attend only a couple of sessions a week at pre-school. A reputation for unpredictability or inappropriate or violent reactions can set a pattern for social exclusion at an early age – not being invited to parties or other children's houses for tea. Other children can be extremely unnerved when one of their peers 'loses it' and they become wary of approaching them. Staff in the setting need to be alert to situations arising and be prepared to talk to parents and carers about their child's problems early on to try and reduce the likelihood of difficulties escalating.

Another trigger time for some children's behaviour to deteriorate in the school setting is around snack time, which in most early years settings is regarded as an enjoyable time – well structured and organised – with a chance to stop and socialise. The tendency for a lot of families today to allow everyone to 'graze' or pick and choose their times for eating, and rarely sitting down all together to eat, has meant that snack and mealtimes in an education setting can be a completely alien activity for some children. Just remaining on a chair and eating a piece of apple offered to them from a big plate while sitting fairly close to another person can be quite a challenge if the young child is used to eating in front of a television, lying down or leaning back on a sofa. Again turn taking, not touching other people's food and waiting until everyone is served and finished before going back to a chosen activity are skills that many children do not learn in the home. If a child has major problems with this part of the school day, staff need to be prepared to discuss this with the parents and carers (who may well be expecting the setting to be the main instructors for 'table manners') and talk through ways of explaining to their child when they are at home the need for learning how to eat with others and why it is important.

Much has been written in the press about family breakdown and the effect it has on the children in the family. All good educational settings are aware of the needs of children who are upset by family circumstances changing, and they will be more than prepared to give the child extra time or a quiet place with a favourite toy or book so that they can have some reflection space, and to provide a trusted adult to keep an extra eye open for signs of distress. It is often the case with younger children that it is the uncertainty of the daily routine at home that makes the school appear to be a secure and comforting place to be, and it is common for children to play happily and sociably while they are there. Staff will often comment that any problems seem to arise once the parents and carers start to arrive to collect their children at the end of the session, and some children become overly anxious if they are not totally clear who will be coming to pick them up. Shared care between parents who are no longer living together usually works very well but children, of any age, need to be assured of the exact arrangements that have been made. Most children can cope easily with the odd change to drop-off and pick-up arrangements but if their arrival and departure from school become fraught with uncertainty and argument their behaviour in school can seriously be altered with poor attention, anxiety and sometimes aggression becoming noticeable. Parents need to be alerted as soon as possible that their child is being affected by uncertain or last-minute changes so that they can make more definite arrangements or provide the setting with mobile telephone numbers or alternative adult contact names to reduce the possibility of the child feeling bewildered and upset at being the last to be collected.

Another factor which sometimes comes into play when families split up or remix is the influence of new siblings, including perhaps teenagers whose needs and lifestyles can impress a youngster. The sort of language used between teenagers and their friends in person or on the telephone can be completely inappropriate for the ears of younger children. Many younger children seem to be able to grasp that there is a difference between home and school and modify their vocabulary accordingly and would never dream of 'swearing' in a school setting. However, others do not easily adjust to different settings and will use inappropriate (and sometimes shocking to the ears of staff and other children) words just because an older child in the house uses them in ordinary conversation. Parents and carers need to be alerted by staff if their child's language or demeanour deteriorates so that they can address the issue. This will give them the opportunity to think about how to set standards at home or at least talk to their child about the need to be 'polite' at school.

Parents and carers are the major influences in any child's life, and communication channels between home and educational establishments need to be maintained and, as far as possible, kept positive so that children do not become confused by conflicting standards. Setting up regular meetings or open days and social events are useful ways to encourage the sharing of concerns and of ensuring that children gain the most from their experiences.

Nurture groups

Nurture groups were developed to help children who for one reason or another had had poor nurturing and parenting or had missed out on these experiences that are vital for development in early childhood.

Nurture groups started in Inner London in Hackney in 1969 in response to high levels of stress in primary schools. Referrals to special units at that time had reached unmanageable levels and staff turnover in some areas had reached 50 per cent.

Children with emotional and behavioural difficulties are unable to progress in the child-centred format of mainstream schools in spite of the best efforts of teachers. This was recognised by the nurture group movement and still has implications for our child-initiated learning focus in early years settings now.

Most nurture groups are in infant schools but are becoming more common in primary and in secondary schools. The classic nurture group consists of six to eight children, situated in a classroom in a mainstream school with a teacher and an assistant in charge. Specific training to run a nurture group is recommended in order to understand the values and ideas that underpin the movement. The nurture group is supported and understood by all staff and is a 'whole school' issue. Children are registered in their base classes and return to them for specific sessions; for example, if a child is particularly good at PE, he takes part in this with his peers in the base class. Children can return to the nurture group when they need to.

The key elements of a nurture group are to build trust and acceptance, to deliver secure routines, to listen to children, to relate to the child as a parent would and to help the child to make sense of the world. The fundamental idea is that it is a small class providing a safe, structured, predictable environment in which a child is given opportunities to make up for early missed nurturing experiences. The physical environment should reflect the general appearance and atmosphere of a home. Typically, there is a kitchen area, dining table and soft furnishings as well as items such as a full-length mirror.

The teacher and the teaching assistant model positive relationships with the emphasis being on developing language and communication skills. Children work one to one, in pairs or in small groups with an adult. Achievement is raised by carefully targeted teaching and learning opportunities.

Parents are encouraged to work in partnership with the school.

The National Curriculum is taught in the nurture group but it is delivered taking account of the child's developmental level. The effects of setting up a nurture group in a school with high levels of need have been positive. Not only does it raise the levels of achievement of those children who attend the group but it raises standards of achievement across the whole school.

Who can benefit from an inclusion in a nurture group

- Children with a history of poor or disrupted parenting

- Children with seriously underdeveloped emotional/social/language skills

- Children with underdeveloped attention and listening skills

- Children who have limited play skills

- Children who are unable to share, cooperate and play collaboratively

- Children who have few friends

- Children who disrupt other children

- Children whose fundamental emotional and social needs have not been met

- Children who have restricted access to the curriculum

- Children who attend nurture groups will have most or all of the characteristics listed above. The nature of these difficulties will be severe and impact upon the child's ability to achieve and to make progress. The nurture group gives these children opportunities to develop an understanding of their own emotional needs and those of other children.

The Boxall profile

The Boxall profile is a powerful aid for intervening effectively in the education of children who are failing in school. First published in 1984 by the Inner London Education Authority, the profile and guidelines for its use were devised by Marjorie Boxall and her colleagues for use in schools with nurture groups.*

The Boxall profile provides a framework for the structured observation of children in the classroom. Its purpose was to provide a means of assessing areas of difficulty for severely disadvantaged children. It enables teachers to plan focused intervention. It enables nurture groups to succeed in helping to keep children at risk of exclusion in mainstream education and to make good progress.

The Boxall profile is a two-part checklist completed by a teacher who knows the child in class. It provides a framework for precise assessment of children failing in school. It helps to plan focused assessments. It is easy and quick, constructive, and avoids labelling. It helps discover what lies behind behaviour.

Nurture groups have a proven track record of reducing exclusions where they are in place in schools.

*Bennathan, Marion and Boxall, Marjorie, *The Boxall Profile: A Guide to Effective Intervention in the Education of Pupils with Emotional and Behavioural Difficulties. Handbook for Teachers*, London: Inner London Education Authority, 1984.

APPENDICES

Abuse: key symptoms

Sexual abuse: key symptoms

ADHD: key symptoms

ADHD checklist

Conduct disorder: key symptoms

SEBD: key symptoms

Depression: key symptoms

Mental disorders: key symptoms

Obsessive-compulsive disorder: key symptoms

Weekly recording sheet

Incident form

Pupil profile

Guidelines for working with your child at home

ABUSE: KEY SYMPTOMS

- Constant crying in babies/children

- Unexplained bruising/injuries

- Children who are withdrawn

- Children who present with dirty/smelly clothing

- Children who are hungry all the time

- Children who are overdressed in hot weather

- Children who are left home alone

- Children who are left in unsafe situations

- Children who are constantly 'put down', sworn at, insulted or humiliated

- Children who seem afraid of a particular adult or adults

- Children who demonstrate unexplained changes of emotions

- Children who show sexual knowledge that is inappropriate for their age

- Children who live with addicts

From Angela Glenn, Alicia Helps and Jacquie Cousins, *Managing Extreme Behaviours in the Early Years*, London: Routledge © 2009 Angela Glenn, Alicia Helps and Jacquie Cousins

SEXUAL ABUSE: KEY SYMPTOMS

- Pain, itching, bleeding in genital areas

- Urinary tract infections

- Discomfort walking/sitting

- Sexually transmitted infections

- Children who become unusually quiet or withdrawn

- Children who have difficulty concentrating

- Children who show unexpected fear of a particular adult or adults

- Children who demonstrate sexually explicit knowledge/language especially if not appropriate to their age

- Children who describe having a 'special' friendship with an adult

Note

Important:

- It is very hard to be 100 per cent sure that abuse has taken place.

- In some cases the above signs may have a completely reasonable explanation.

- There may be other things that cause concern.

- Do not keep concerns to yourself.

- Contact NSPCC (trained child protection officers will be able to give advice), Health Visitor, Teacher, GP, Social Worker.

From Angela Glenn, Alicia Helps and Jacquie Cousins, *Managing Extreme Behaviours in the Early Years*, London: Routledge © 2009 Angela Glenn, Alicia Helps and Jacquie Cousins

ADHD: KEY SYMPTOMS

Inattention

- Inability to sustain attention closely
- Distractability
- Procrastination
- Losing and forgetting
- Not finishing things
- Not listening
- Disorganisation

Hyperactivity

- Fidgetiness
- Restlessness
- On the go constantly
- Plays noisily
- Talkativeness

Impulsiveness

- Verbal impulsivity
- Physical impulsivity
- The key symptoms significantly interfere with daily life

Associated difficulties

- Self-esteem
- Social skills
- Relationships
- Time management
- Organisation
- Motivation
- Physical symptoms
- Short-term memory
- Learning
- Hypersensitivity
- Vulnerability
- Dogmatism
- Insatiability
- High/low IQ

From Angela Glenn, Alicia Helps and Jacquie Cousins, *Managing Extreme Behaviours in the Early Years*, London: Routledge © 2009 Angela Glenn, Alicia Helps and Jacquie Cousins

ADHD CHECKLIST

Checklist ADHD	Not at all	Just a little	Quite often	All the time
Often fidgets or squirms in seat				
Has difficulty remaining in seat				
Is easily distracted				
Has difficulty waiting in line or taking turns				
Often blurts out answers				
Has difficulty following instructions				
Has difficulty sustaining attention to tasks				
Often shifts from one uncompleted task to another				
Has difficulty playing quietly				
Often talks excessively				
Often interrupts or intrudes on others				
Often loses things necessary for tasks				
Often engages in physically dangerous activities without considering consequences				

Note

It is vital that checklists are used with caution. The most important thing to remember is that very young children all demonstrate these behaviours to varying degrees. The child with ADHD often has all or most of these behaviour traits. As with other disorders, ADHD is a continuum.

It is important to note whether and how the behaviour is impacting upon the child's ability to access the curriculum and whether the child is making progress.

These symptoms need to be present in more than one environment.

From Angela Glenn, Alicia Helps and Jacquie Cousins, *Managing Extreme Behaviours in the Early Years*, London: Routledge © 2009 Angela Glenn, Alicia Helps and Jacquie Cousins

CONDUCT DISORDER: KEY SYMPTOMS

- Aggression towards people or animals

- Conduct causing property loss or damage

- Deceitfulness or theft

- Serious rule violation

From Angela Glenn, Alicia Helps and Jacquie Cousins, *Managing Extreme Behaviours in the Early Years*, London: Routledge © 2009 Angela Glenn, Alicia Helps and Jacquie Cousins

SEBD: KEY SYMPTOMS

- Difficulty forming friendships

- Appearing preoccupied, difficulty engaging with activities

- Difficulty staying on task

- Difficulty taking part in group activities

- Tears or tantrums

- Psychosomatic illnesses

- Low self-esteem

- Becoming bully or victim of bullying

- Aggression and disruption

- Difficulty conforming to rules and routines

- Excessive attention seeking or clinginess

- School phobia

- Underachievement

From Angela Glenn, Alicia Helps and Jacquie Cousins, *Managing Extreme Behaviours in the Early Years*, London: Routledge © 2009 Angela Glenn, Alicia Helps and Jacquie Cousins

DEPRESSION: KEY SYMPTOMS

- Internalises feelings

- Moodiness

- Seems miserable and unhappy for most of the time

- Withdrawal, avoidance of family and friends

- Self-critical

- Feelings of guilt

- Persistent hopelessness

- Difficulty concentrating

- Tiredness

- Comfort eating

- Loss of appetite

- Episodes of self-harm

- Wanting to die

- Drug/alcohol/substance abuse

- Irritability

From Angela Glenn, Alicia Helps and Jacquie Cousins, *Managing Extreme Behaviours in the Early Years*, London: Routledge © 2009 Angela Glenn, Alicia Helps and Jacquie Cousins

MENTAL DISORDERS: KEY SYMPTOMS

- Drug/alcohol/substance abuse
- Inability to cope with daily activities
- Changes to sleeping or eating
- Excessive complaints about physical ailments
- Defying authority
- Skipping school
- Stealing or damaging property
- Intense fear of gaining weight
- Long-lasting negative moods
- Poor appetite
- Thoughts about death
- Frequent outbursts of anger
- Changes in performance
- Loss of interest in friends
- Increase in time spent alone
- Excessive worry or anxiety
- Hyperactivity
- Nightmares or night terrors
- Frequent temper tantrums
- Hearing voices or hallucinations

From Angela Glenn, Alicia Helps and Jacquie Cousins, *Managing Extreme Behaviours in the Early Years*, London: Routledge © 2009 Angela Glenn, Alicia Helps and Jacquie Cousins

OBSESSIVE–COMPULSIVE DISORDER: KEY SYMPTOMS

- Ritualistic behaviour that is upsetting, takes a long time, interferes with daily life

- Unreasonable fears about harming self or others

- Inordinate concern for order

- Fears that activities or objects are not safe

- Behaviours that are frequent, automatic, distressing and difficult to control or get rid of

From Angela Glenn, Alicia Helps and Jacquie Cousins, *Managing Extreme Behaviours in the Early Years*, London: Routledge © 2009 Angela Glenn, Alicia Helps and Jacquie Cousins

WEEKLY RECORDING SHEET

Name: **Week commencing:**

Time	Mon	Tue	Wed	Thur	Fri
9.00–9.15					
9.15–9.30					
9.30–9.45					
9.45–10.00					
10.00–10.15					
10.15–10.30					
10.30–10.45					
10.45–11.00					
11.00–11.15					
11.15–11.30					
11.30–11.45					
11.45–12.00					
12.00–12.15					
12.15–12.30					
12.30–12.45					
12.45–1.00					
1.00–1.15					
1.15–1.30					
1.30–1.45					
1.45–2.00					
2.00–2.15					
2.15–2.30					
2.30–2.45					
2.45–3.00					
3.00–3.15					
3.15–3.30					

1. On task/happy/polite
2. On task
3. Off task/silent
4. Off task/loud
5. Off task/physically aggressive

From Angela Glenn, Alicia Helps and Jacquie Cousins, *Managing Extreme Behaviours in the Early Years*, London: Routledge © 2009 Angela Glenn, Alicia Helps and Jacquie Cousins

INCIDENT FORM

(To be completed whenever a child acts in a way that endangers him/ herself or others or when direct physical intervention is necessary)

Name of child:

Date, time and duration of incident:

Name(s) of staff involved:

Brief details of the incident (context, trigger for behaviour, where it occurred):

Follow-up action:

Signature: Head of establishment

…………………………………………..

Parent/Carer ……………………………………………………………

From Angela Glenn, Alicia Helps and Jacquie Cousins, *Managing Extreme Behaviours in the Early Years*, London: Routledge © 2009 Angela Glenn, Alicia Helps and Jacquie Cousins

PUPIL PROFILE

Pupil _____ **School** _____

Date completed_____ by _____

Positive attributes

Please rate each of the following behaviours on the scale:
0 – No cause for concern, 1 – Very mild cause for concern, 2 – Mild cause for concern, 3 – Cause for concern, 4 – Serious cause for concern, 5 – Very serious cause for concern

From Angela Glenn, Alicia Helps and Jacquie Cousins, *Managing Extreme Behaviours in the Early Years*, London: Routledge © 2009 Angela Glenn, Alicia Helps and Jacquie Cousins

A – Academic behaviour

	0	1	2	3	4	5
A1 Following written instructions						
A2 Following verbal instructions						
A3 Setting to work						
A4 Working without direct supervision						
A5 Class work: written						
A6 Class work: practical						
A7 Class work: discussion						
A8 Classwork: group work						
A9 Task completion						
A10 Presentation of work						

B – Rules and routine

	0	1	2	3	4	5
B1 Following the rules of the classroom						
B2						
B3						
B4						
B5						
B6 Hanging up coat/bag*						
B7 Entering/leaving room*						
B8 Starting/finishing activity*						
B9 Distributing materials						
B10 Seeking/waiting for teacher assistance*						

B2 to B5: please insert 4 rules of your classroom and rate pupil compliance.
* Delete as appropriate.

From Angela Glenn, Alicia Helps and Jacquie Cousins, *Managing Extreme Behaviours in the Early Years*, London: Routledge © 2009 Angela Glenn, Alicia Helps and Jacquie Cousins

C – Verbal/noisy behaviours

	0	1	2	3	4	5
C1 Taps/bangs on desk/table*						
C2 Moves furniture						
C3 Calls/shouts to teacher*						
C4 Inappropriate comments to teacher						
C5 Talks/shouts to pupils*						
C6 Talks/mutters to self*						
C7 Sings inappropriately						
C8 Whistles inappropriately						
C9 Makes non-verbal noises						
C10 Giggles/laughs inappropriately*						

* Delete as appropriate.

D – In seat/out of seat behaviours

	0	1	2	3	4	5
D1 Turns/rocks/fidgets in seat*						
D2 Sits out of position in seat						
D3 Stands up out of seat						
D4 Changes seat						
D5 Lies/crawls on floor*						
D6 Stamps feet						
D7 Climbs on furniture						
D8 Moves from seat/walks about*						
D9 Runs about classroom						
D10 Leaves class without permission						

* Delete as appropriate.

From Angela Glenn, Alicia Helps and Jacquie Cousins, *Managing Extreme Behaviours in the Early Years*, London: Routledge © 2009 Angela Glenn, Alicia Helps and Jacquie Cousins

E – Aggressive/destructive behaviours

	0	1	2	3	4	5
Pupil oriented						
Ep1 Strikes other pupil(s)						
Ep2 Kicks other pupil(s)						
Ep3 Pushes other pupil(s)						
Ep4 Trips other pupil(s)						
Ep5 Bites other pupil(s)						
Ep6 Scratches other pupil(s)						
Ep7 Pinches other pupil(s)						
Ep8 Physically/verbally threatens other pupil(s)*						
Ep9 Damages property of other pupil(s)						
Ep10 Takes property of other pupil(s)						
Teacher oriented						
Et1 Argues with teacher						
Et2 Hits out at teacher						
Et3 Cheeky to teacher						
Et4 Physically/verbally threatens teacher*						
Et5 Makes inappropriate gestures						
Et6 Spits/other anti-social behaviour*						
Et7 Uses offensive language						
Et8 Throws equipment/books*						
Et9 Writes/scribbles on others' books/ property*						
Et10 Damages others'/school property*						

* Delete as appropriate.

From Angela Glenn, Alicia Helps and Jacquie Cousins, *Managing Extreme Behaviours in the Early Years*, London: Routledge © 2009 Angela Glenn, Alicia Helps and Jacquie Cousins

F – Social/emotional adjustments

	0	1	2	3	4	5
F1 Not popular/disliked by other pupils*						
F2 Often worried						
F3 Tends to be solitary						
F4 Irritable/loses temper easily*						
F5 Appears unhappy/miserable/ tearful/distressed*						
F6 Sucks thumb/fingers/bites nails/ fingers/clothes*						
F7 Tearful/over-anxious at new things/ situations*						
F8 Over-fussy/particular*						
F9 Passive/apathetic*						
F10 Unhappy/tearful on arrival at school/school refusal*						

* Delete as appropriate

GUIDELINES FOR WORKING WITH YOUR CHILD AT HOME

- Understand your child's particular strengths and weaknesses.

- Don't overwhelm your child.

- Maintain close contact with teachers.

- Work with the 'whole child' – self-esteem is critical.

- Clear the area – reduce distractions.

- Recognise your own emotions and needs.

- Take five minutes to prepare yourself.

- Begin and end the work with fun.

- Be positive.

- Be patient.

- Break work into short periods of time.

- Be flexible with tasks but consistent with expectations.

- Find the time of day when work is most productive.

From Angela Glenn, Alicia Helps and Jacquie Cousins, *Managing Extreme Behaviours in the Early Years*, London: Routledge © 2009 Angela Glenn, Alicia Helps and Jacquie Cousins

GLOSSARY

ADHD	Attention Deficit Hyperactivity Disorder
ASD	Autistic Spectrum Disorder
OCD	Obsessive–Compulsive Disorder
SEBD	Social, Emotional and Behavioural Difficulties